GOOD NEWS STUDIES

Consulting Editor: Robert J. Karris, O.F.M.

Volume 8

A Galilean Rabbi And His Bible

Jesus' Use of the Interpreted Scripture of His Time

by

Bruce D. Chilton

 Michael Glazier, Inc.
Wilmington, Delaware

ABOUT THE AUTHOR:

Bruce D. Chilton teaches New Testament at Sheffield University in England. He holds degrees from Bard College, the General Theological Seminary and Cambridge University. Among his publications are *God in Strength: Jesus' Announcement of the Kingdom*; and *The Glory of Israel: The Theology and Provenience of the Isaiah Targum*. He is also Executive Editor of *Journal for the Study of the New Testament* and its series of monographs and collected essays.

First published in 1984 by Michael Glazier, Inc.
1723 Delaware Avenue, Wilmington, Delaware 19806

©1984 by Bruce D. Chilton. All rights reserved.

Library of Congress Catalog Card Number: 83-82666
International Standard Book Number:
  Good News Studies: 0-89453-290-1
  A GALILEAN RABBI
    0-89453-374-6 (Michael Glazier, Inc.)

Typography by Susan H. Pickett

Printed in the United States of America

Contents

For Odile —
un cadeau pour le 28 juin et le 3 juillet.

FOREWORD

It is my privilege to introduce Professor Bruce Chilton and this study to a North American audience.

Professor Chilton, who teaches in the department of biblical studies at the University of Sheffield in Britain, received his doctorate in New Testment from Cambridge University in 1976. The title of his dissertation, which was published in 1979, is *God in Strength: Jesus' Announcement of the Kingdom*. As the Bibliography at the end of this monograph graphically attests, Professor Chilton has published widely since receiving his doctorate. The bulk of his research has been in the area of the historical Jesus. And this research, in turn, has been the reason for his pursuit of the study of the ancient Targum on Isaiah.

This monograph is very rich and deals with the major areas which have occupied Chilton's time over the past ten years: how the Isaiah Targum allows researchers and ordinary readers of the Gospels to understand more readily the preaching of Jesus of Nazareth. To those concerns Chilton has added a further area, namely, how Jesus' fulfillment use of the Old Testament may inform Christian faith and preaching today.

Professor Chilton writes clearly as he addresses the question of the Judaism contemporary with Jesus of Nazareth. The Isaiah Targum and the interpretative traditions embedded in it are examples of this Judaism and help explain Jesus' use of the Old Testament in his preaching and teaching. Chilton writes provocatively as he explores the contemporary meaning of the fact that Jesus preached the way he did.

In brief, the author has produced a study which will inform and inspire, a study which will contribute much to the pursuit of the historical Jesus, a study which will serve as a provocative textbook for courses in Christology and in Gospel criticism. He is to be congratulated on his accomplishment.

North American readers may wonder whether the issues addressed in this monograph reflect concerns peculiar to Britain. A cursory look at the new work of John Dominic Crossan on *The Aphoristic Jesus* and of James Breech on *The Silence of Jesus* will show that Chilton's concerns are North American concerns, too. And those familiar with current North American research in the area of hermeneutics, e.g., the research of Sandra Schneiders, will recognize the same issues as those treated by Chilton in his discussion of the contemporary significance of Jesus' use of Scripture.

This study treats international issues of contemporary Gospel research and deserves an international hearing.

Robert J. Karris, O.F.M.
Catholic Theological Union, Chicago

PREFACE

Is exegesis necessarily boring? Recent trends in New Testament study might lead one to say, "yes." In an attempt to enliven an ailing discipline, professional scholars tend either to say more and more about smaller and smaller bits of the biblical text, or to generalize globally about the significance of the canon as a whole without grounding their discussion in what the text actually says. Why is that? I would like to suggest two reasons.

First, New Testament study has become, as has frequently been said, an academic ghetto. Despite recent advances in the study of, for example, Judaism, Gnosticism and the entire process of interpreting a text, books and articles continue to be written as if the New Testament were in a world of its own, and not the product of an age and a people that we can understand fully only by looking at documents other than the New Testament. Of course, a similar isolationism might be said to afflict experts in the three fields mentioned above, some of whom are simplistic and defective in their understanding of the New Testament, but that only reinforces the point that we are the victims of an unfruitful specialization.

Second, there is a strong feeling among students that somehow biblical interpretation has become too technical, that the New Testament demands an evaluation of its truth claims, and not just comments on how the text got to be the way it is. An eloquent appeal to this effect has recently been made by Nicholas Lash (1981). But it is one thing to thirst for convincing statements about the significance of a work, and quite another to provide them: far too frequently, theologians make truth claims in the name of the Bible without relating them clearly to the text.

Both of these difficulties have been on my mind during the years required to complete the present study, and while I have been preparing the manuscript itself. Accordingly, I have had two main aims.

The first is to present historical evidence and evaluation which help us to understand Jesus and his followers. My conviction is that the importance of the Aramaic Targum to Isaiah has not been appreciated by New Testament scholars, with the result that we have simply missed certain key points in Jesus' preaching. Part one of this volume explains the position of the Targum in Jewish literature and in recent study; part two shows how the Targum illuminates certain sayings of Jesus in a significant way. Part one is intentionally of an introductory nature, and is designed to offer a general orientation in the field to those who are not familiar with the study of rabbinic literature. Inevitably, part two has been written with precise reference to evidence: we are talking here, after all, about exactly what Jesus said and meant. Nonetheless, every attempt has been made to avoid technicality, and any assumption that the reader enjoys specialist knowledge.

My second purpose has been to draw attention to the fact that this fresh historical evidence does not just amount to an interesting collection of bits and pieces. In the course of the present study, a definite pattern began to emerge, a pattern which permits us to see the way Jesus used the Bible of his day. The pattern can be seen to evolve as one reads through part two, and in part three Jesus' style of preaching as a whole is described. In a sense, this amounts to nothing more than spelling out the implications of part two, and is a natural consequence of our historical inquiry. On the other hand, part three also uses the preaching style of Jesus as an occasion for developing a view of how the Bible can be read critically and at the same time in the context of faith. Issues of a hermeneutical nature are therefore raised and addressed.

For those who have kept history and theology in separate compartments, the structure of this book will no doubt seem odd. If that is so, I would reply that the oddity of my approach is no greater than, and in kind no different from, the oddity of Christian faith, in which the particulars of the biblical text, in their reference to human events from the past, are related to a God who is conceived of as transcendent and unchanging. In this volume, I invite readers, no matter what their belief or lack of belief, to see how Jesus used his Bible in order to speak directly of God. To anyone with a sense of history, the matter is interesting. To those of us who are possessed also of a sense of God, it is crucial.

The bulk of this volume was written at Münster at the Forschungsstelle Antike und Christentum. I extend my thanks to my host, Karl Heinrich Rengstorf, and to the Minister für Wissenschaft und Forschung, who made an academically rewarding visit financially possible. C.F.D. Moule has shouldered the burden of friendship in reading the manuscript through: when the reader suffers from any error or density, he can comfort himself with the thought that Prof. Moule spared him much worse. The dedication, I hope, will not be cryptic to those who are intended to understand it. Others might gather the meaning from Genesis 29:1-12.

Part One

INTRODUCTION

1. Jesus and Judaism

Anyone who wishes to understand the New Testament is, consciously or not, a student of early Judaism. When we speak of "early Judaism," we refer to the religious movement which survived the effective demise of Israel as a theocratic state and was the precedent of rabbinic Judaism. Before the first century B.C., Israel had been governed by institutions believed to have divine warrant. Temple and king together enjoyed scriptural authorization (see, for example, 1 Kings 9:1-5) and — although disruptive breaks and unusual accommodations occurred in the history of both —Israel naturally looked to these two institutions as the guarantors of national identity and of divinely willed prosperity. The country might nearly tear itself apart with disputes concerning proper kingship, the correct conduct of the cult, and the balance of power between the priest and monarch, but that God willed an Israel ordered by both was essentially axiomatic. The axiom endured the rise of Assyrian power, which resulted in the demolition of the northern kingdom (in the eighth century). It even endured the Babylonian deportation in the sixth century: Cyrus the Persian triumphed over Israel's captors, and royal and cultic institutions — albeit limited in scope — were permitted to function again in Jerusalem. Israel suffered further infringements on its autonomy as it fell alternatively under the sway of the Egyptian Ptolemies and the Syrian Seleucids, dynastic successors to Alexander the Great. Such infringements did not dampen Israel's faith in its destiny as a theocratic state. When the Seleucid Antiochus IV Epiphanes attempted to alter Temple sacrifice itself in his programme of Hellenization (167 B.C.), he faced open revolt, and the consequent establishment of Jewish autonomy in the form of the Hasmoneans represented a vigorous affirmation of the cult and the monarchy as Israel's guardians. Nascent Roman hegemony also left Israel intact, but when the struggle for preeminence among Hasmonean pretenders degenerated into civil war, Pompey entered Jerusalem (in 63 B.C.). Once Roman power in the area — challenged by Parthia — had been consolidated, Herod governed the territory of Israel as a vassal king (from 37 B.C.).

Since 721 B.C., when the inhabitants of the northern kingdom were deported by the Assyrians, "Israel" had effectively been Judah, the largest territory in the south. But before Pompey's invasion, Judah had consistently attempted to secure the territories and prestige that had once belonged to Israel as a whole. In the second century, John Hyrcanus had to a remarkable extent succeeded in this endeavour; he won lands as far north as Galilee and as far south as Idumea. Even before the deportation of 721, Israel had been divided into northern and southern kingdoms by a dispute over the legitimate kingship, so that the ambition and vigour of John Hyrcanus and the Hasmonean family as a whole appear all the more striking in their historical context. After the energy of the family wasted itself in internal wrangling, and Pompey entered Jerusalem, the situation altered, although notable and violent resurgences of nationalism in later periods attest the power of the old dream of Israel's autonomy. The monarchy had ceased, and high priestly office came largely to be in the gift of the ruler appointed by Rome. Judah, once the pre-eminent territory in Israel and the engine of national pride, now provided the geographical centre of Judaism, a religious movement based on the application of God's will in Torah (that is, "law") to the life of the community and of the individual. The appeal to Torah in the face of national calamity was natural: what God gave Moses on Sinai was understood to express the essence of Israel's identity, and one naturally looked to this supreme gift when that identity was threatened. Moreover, this recourse to the law in times of national stress had an important precedent. Nehemiah 8 describes the work of Ezra and his associates during the difficult period after the Babylonian exile when those who returned to Jerusalem attempted to re-establish their national institutions. Ezra, called a priest, is said to bring the law before an assembly of "all who had understanding to hear" (v. 2); he read aloud while the people listened (vv. 3f.), and his associates helped them to understand (v. 7). In what appears a summary of their ministry, v. 8 reads, "And they read from the book, God's law, while he instructed and gave the sense, and they gave understanding in what was read." (This is a difficult passage; I have construed the Hebrew text on the basis of the translation offered in the ancient Greek translation called the Septuagint, at 2 Esdras 18:8). When, at a much later period, the rabbis looked back in history to describe their own origins, they spoke of Ezra as the writer of the biblical books of Ezra and Nehemiah, and of some of the genealogies in Chronicles. (The reference is in the Babylonian Talmud, which will be discussed below; it appears in Baba Bathra 15a.). In the same passage, a group called the men of the great synagogue is mentioned, to which the writing of Ezekiel and of the Minor Prophets is ascribed. At the same time, Ezra and the men of the great synagogue are considered the founders of the rabbinic movement as a whole. By the time the Talmud was produced (in the fifth century A.D.), then, the rabbis saw Ezra and the men of the great synagogue, not only as their precursors, but as intimately involved with the substance of scripture, along with its interpretation. The rabbinic conviction that there was a continuous movement which linked them directly to the last of the prophets is succinctly expressed in the opening of a tractate from the Mishnah (which will also be discussed below), called Avoth: "Moses received the Torah at Sinai and transmitted it to Joshua, Joshua to the elders, and the elders to the prophets, and the prophets to the men of the great synagogue." (There are various versions of this tractate, which can be dated in different periods; this statement is a part of the earliest version, datable within the second century.) Torah, therefore, is for the representatives of this movement "law," not in the sense of a desiccated code of behaviour, but in the sense of the guidance offered by God to his people through its exposition generation after generation. Precisely because the Torah was not merely a legalistic formula, the rabbis sought to discover in it the living principles given by God through which his people might survive and flourish.

The last point must be appreciated fully by any student of Judaism; there is a lamentable and persistent tendency to imagine that the rabbis were dry legalists simply because they expended immense time and energy in applying Torah to aspects of life which do not happen to seem "relevant" to us. The Talmud, although compiled centuries after the destruction of the Temple, does indeed devote a tractate to sacrifices and the day of atonement (Yoma), and this is but one example from the many which could be cited of its characteristic absorption with the Torah in all its variety, no matter what the contemporary circumstances, as the ethical, devotional and intellectual centre of a life of fidelity to the Lord. In this case, Talmud builds on the Mishnah (which developed earlier, nearer the time of the Temple) and reflects the continuing importance of the day of atonement tradition in the Jewish calendar, even after Temple sacrifice could not be offered. But such care and attention to tradition can only be styled as legalism when the tradition is no longer developed creatively to meet changing conditions, and precisely such a concern for development is at the heart of rabbinic Judaism. The dialectical format of much rabbinic literature, in which the views of different rabbis are set out, distinctions between them observed and a final position attained, attests the dynamic understanding of tradition which the rabbis implicitly shared. To some, of course, rabbinic Judaism may appear legalistic just because it insists on the precise discussion of opinions from the past, although for some reason the charge is not commonly leveled against Christianity, Islam, or the great, traditionally based religions of the East. Such attempts to dismiss rabbinic Judaism with a label say much more about our own times than about the theology of the rabbis, and reveal an antipathy to Jewish thinking which is inconsistent with the historian's duty to describe the phenomenon he is studying in its own context before he attempts to evaluate it.

Eventually, rabbinic discussion came to be conducted in definite academies, which were organized and maintained for the purpose. Once the academies had emerged, rabbinic Judaism came into existence, in that Jewish religion was characterized by professional religious discussion. To such academies we owe the immense wealth of rabbinic literature, and the very survival of Judaism. In 70 A.D., the Jewish people received a much more cruel shock than even the substantive usurpation of the monarchy by the Romans was: when the Temple was demolished during the initial stages of the occupation under Titus, after the long siege directed by his father Vespasian, the heartbeat of Jewish sacrificial life effectively stopped. With the demise of legitimate monarchy, the Temple had become the remaining focus of Israel's faith. The Temple and proper cultic worship were consuming interests in the first century A.D. Groups such as the Qumran community might withdraw from the Jerusalem cult, but they did so only until its expected reformation according to the will of God. When, on one occasion, Jesus came to Jerusalem, his concern with cultic matters was sufficient to drive him to disrupt what he saw as improper commercial activity (Matthew 21:12-13; Mark 11:15-17; Luke 19:45-46; John 2:13-17). This disruption is conventionally, but too lamely, called the "cleansing" of the Temple: in all the Gospels, after all, Jesus is said to expel (ἐκβάλλειν) the vendors, and in John the additional detail is given that Jesus made a lash from ropes for this purpose (v. 15). Mark adds that Jesus did not permit anyone to carry a vessel through the Temple, and this implies he interrupted regular cultic operations. Taking the hint from Mark, we might call Jesus' act an "occupation' of the Temple, so long as we bear in mind that it was not sufficiently extensive (in time or impact) to warrant military action against Jesus and his followers. Since the Romans provided for the defense of the Temple, which was highly regarded in the Mediterranean world as a holy site, we would require evidence of an immediate military reaction before we could conclude that Jesus' occupation was anything more than an illustrative act (however vehement) by which he intended to demonstrate what he deeply believed was the proper use of the Temple. In an article which appeared nearly twenty years ago, but which has not attracted the attention it merits, Victor Eppstein (1964) cited the rabbinic evidence which shows that, under the high priest Caiaphas (cf. Matthew 26:3, 57; Luke 3:2; John 11:49; 18:13, 14, 24, 28; Acts 4:6) there was considerable controversy over the siting of cultically related commercial activity. The extent of rabbinic discussion relating to sacrificial matters clearly demonstrates that even after 70 the cultic interest of the rabbis remained.

With the demolition of the Temple, whose precincts had also served as a magnet for such teachers as Jesus and those with whom he debated, a characteristic centre of Jewish devotion was destroyed. Sacrificial continuity was broken; an important economic focus for Jewish piety was effaced; the foundation of priestly aristocracy, which had provided such leadership as Israel enjoyed, was removed. Most crucially, the sacrificial praxis which, in their own minds, related Jews to God, had ceased. What, now, did it mean to be a child of the covenant? What took the place of the daily Temple rites and the great pilgrim feasts, which had drawn Jews — and not only Jews — from all over the civilized world? In an anciently attributed saying in Mishnah (Avoth 1:2), the world itself is said to rely on three things: Torah, Temple service, and deeds of faithful love. A legend is told about a rabbi named Johanan ben Zakkai. One day, looking at the demolished Temple site, he declared that the atonement once made in the sacrificial cult was still available through deeds of faithful love. To support his case, he cited Hosea 6:6, "I desire faithful love, and not sacrifice." Jesus, according to Matthew (9:13; 12:7), applied this verse to the debate about rules of cleanness and keeping sabbath; it appears that the rabbis, too, developed a more ethical view of obedience to Torah in face of the cataclysm of 70 A.D. (The rabbinic evidence here cited is taken from the magnificent compendium of Paul Billerbeck [1926], discussed below; the legend appears in Avoth de Rabbi Nathan 4.)

"Faithful love" is a noble ideal, but one that requires definition if the phrase is to be more than a slogan, and the rabbis were quite clear as to the definition of ethical behaviour:

> Rabbi Eleazar ben Azariah (a second century rabbi) said, Where there is no Torah, there is no right conduct, where there is no right conduct, there is no Torah (Avoth 3:18).

Torah was now to be the means of Jews' relationship with God; the divine presence (Shekhinah), once felt to be associated with the Temple, was now held to rest on those who discussed the law (Avoth 3:6). Rabbi Johanan ben Zakkai himself understood that the ethical orientation he espoused required grounding in Torah, and his cleverness and wisdom assured the success of the first great post-70 rabbinic academy. The Talmud (Gittin 56a, b) recounts that Johanan realized that death awaited those in besieged Jerusalem. On the advice of his nephew, he pretended to be ill, and then to have died as a consequence; two of his disciples carried him outside the city as a corpse, successfully pleading with some thugs who wished comprehensively to ensure Johanan was dead that it would hearten the Romans to know the body of so great a teacher had been mutilated by his own people. Johanan, safely out of the city, went to Vespasian and hailed him as king; the great general was angry at the implied slight on the majesty of Caesar. Johanan temporized, explaining that Vespasian must be a king for Jerusalem to be delivered into his hand. But the news soon came that Caesar had in fact died and the Romans were looking to Vespasian for leadership. Vespasian now viewed Johanan differently, and offered to grant him a request. Johanan is portrayed as having his answer ready, "Give me Yavneh (a town near Jerusalem) and its wise men, the family group of Rabban Gamaliel, and physicians to heal Rabbi Zadok." The request seems characteristic of the man. Selfless but determined, he wanted the necessary protection, plant and expert personnel to continue and extend the influence of the exposition of Torah, and his demand for a physician reflects the pastoral concern which is a hallmark of rabbinic Judaism. This Talmudic story is an example of haggadah. A haggadah is a narrative designed first of all to illustrate certain principles of Israel's faith: any historical value is incidental. The present story is at least as illustrative of Johanan's basic principles and charming wiliness as it is designed to convey what we would call historical information. In this regard, it might be borne in mind that Josephus also claimed to have acclaimed Vespasian prophetically (cf. *Jewish Wars* III.8:9), and that the story about Johanan has been seen as legendary in recent discussion (cf. Saldarini [1975]). The fact remains, however, that from the modest, somewhat fortuitous beginnings in Yavneh the religious vitality of the Jewish people, so recently subjected to what must have seemed a devastating shock, was restored, redefined, and applied to daily life. Judaism proper was born, and a distinctive form of biblical religion took shape.

The ethos of the Yavneh academy and its successors centred on the exposition of Torah, but Torah in the extended sense which has already been described. The work of the rabbis after 70 A.D. was foundational for what we call Judaism. Judaism proper came into existence because the rabbis, skilled practitioners in the exposition and application of Torah, reconstituted the religious impulses of the Jewish people on the basis of observing Torah, rather than on the basis of a cultic or monarchic understanding of the covenant. The rabbinic programme involved not only theological creativity, but also considerable change at a societal level. The rabbis emerged as the new aristocrats, largely replacing the priesthood (whose interests they nevertheless, as conservers of tradition, maintained). Synagogues, organized originally for the reading of scripture, became centres of the piety and religious discussion which once focused on the Temple, and in some cases academies of professional study were founded. From soon after 70 A.D., in Babylonia as well as in Palestine (see Neusner [1965], [1966]), the rabbis enjoyed the popular support and official toleration which ensured they could promulgate their distinctive understanding of Jewish heritage.

In a productive career devoted to the understanding of the development of rabbinic Judaism, Jacob Neusner has repeatedly stressed the creative aspect of the rabbinic programme. He advocates close attention to the discussion of halakhah (ethical teaching) in the rabbinic academies as it is reflected in Mishnah. For Neusner, the halakhic discussion of the rabbis must be our starting point, because it was the basis of the on-going movement which became known as Judaism (1980, p. 146 and cf. Neusner [1982]). Neusner grants that materials from before the destruction of the Temple are included in rabbinic literature (p. 154), but he rightly observes that the identification of such materials is inferential, since the literature as we know it derives from after that period.

Because the rabbis after 70 A.D. were largely responsible for the emergence of rabbinic Judaism, what are we to say of the period between the full flower of Jewish national religion and the activity of the rabbis? "Early Judaism" is the designation which is now widely used to speak of the period, which saw a ground change in the common understanding of what it meant to be a Jew. In his earlier study, *The Rabbinic Traditions About the Pharisees Before 70* (1971), Neusner concluded that the development of Jewish religion in the one hundred years before 70 A.D. is only sketchily represented in rabbinic literature (III, p. 319). The rabbis indeed referred to the work of predecessors; some — such as Hillel — were contemporaries of Jesus. But, for that matter, they also invoked Ezra and Moses as their authorities, and the point of such attributions was to settle the matter under discussion by means of the claim that the famous predecessor favoured one or another of the contending points of view. The characteristic concern of the rabbis was for the meaning of Torah in their own time; the past was for them a guide to that understanding, not a period of time about which one should write a history for its own sake.

A delightful story from the Talmudic tractate Menaḥoth (29b) illustrates that the rabbis were fully aware of their own creativity as bearers and expositors of Torah. The story, told in the name of Rab, a most influential scholar and founder of an academy in the third century A.D., opens with Moses and God in conversation. God tells Moses that one day a rabbi named Aqiba will arise and expound the Torah. (Aqiba was in fact a second century rabbi who trained many students to be expert interpreters, especially with reference to linguistic details.) Moses asks to see this man, and he is permitted to attend the learned rabbi's school, where he sits near the back of the class. Intellectually, Moses is out of his depth; he cannot follow the erudite discussion of Aqiba and his students. But in the course of the proceedings, one of the students asks Aqiba how he knows of a certain opinion, and he replies, "It is a law given to Moses on Sinai." Moses is both relieved that the law given to him is in fact at the centre of interest and impressed that Aqiba seems to have a first-hand familiarity with it. (In rabbinic discussion, a view is said to be as from Moses on Sinai even when it is not found in the Bible, but has the full warrant of traditional interpretation.) Moses returns to his conference with God, and expresses his astonishment that God should give Torah by his hand when there is a man of Aqiba's learning in prospect. God replies, "Be silent, for such is my decree."

This haggadah from Menaḥoth is obviously designed more to illuminate theological or ethical points than to report historically on the events it recounts. The gist of this tale is clear enough: Aqiba's learning conveys the Torah in a way comparable to the teaching of Moses himself. That such a conviction was current in the New Testament period is shown by Matthew 23:2, where, in a saying of Jesus, the scribes and Pharisees are said to sit "on Moses' seat." The

Torah, for the rabbis, was not only what was written in the alleged books of Moses, but also what was expounded orally by masters such as Aqiba. Torah was a living and developing tradition which, as set down in Talmud, touched almost every aspect of individual and community life. In explaining the transition of Jewish religion from the national institution of the biblical period to the Torah-based devotion of the post-biblical period, we have turned naturally to the Talmud as the most expressive exponent of the later movement. Talmud is the most carefully cut jewel in the crown of rabbinic Judaism, the outcome of centuries of discussion about Torah which probably attained a form which we would identify closely with the Talmudic text we know in the fifth century A.D. But no matter how valuable Talmud may be in conveying rabbinic Judaism, a question must be raised at this point: what justification is there for reading the Talmud's picture of devotion to Torah back into the efforts of Jews in the first century to maintain their faith in the face of national dissolution? No historian can lightly assume that the attitudes and movements of a period are to be understood by referring to documents which post-date that period by some five centuries. This obvious point is worth stressing, because a recent popular book by Geza Vermes (1973) undertakes to understand Jesus in the context of Talmudic Judaism, although the work is subtitled, *A Historian's Reading of the Gospels*. Such attempts beg the basic question, to which we will now turn: what relation has rabbinic Judaism and its literature to the early Judaism of Jesus' period?

From the second century A.D., the rabbis began deliberately to compile the opinions of such great authorities as R. Aqiba in a comprehensive way. These compilations, mentioned in the literature of the Talmudic period and far more systematic than the rough notes of rabbis' views which may have preceded them, fall into three basic categories: midrash, mishnah and targum. A midrash is a collection of the opinions of rabbis arranged in the form of a commentary on a biblical text. Sometimes the material so collected and arranged appears to have been intended by its original speaker as an exegetical comment, but at other times the link with the biblical text seems tenuous, and its inclusion in the midrash more a function of the esteem in which the material was held than of a desire to explain the scripture to which it is attached.

The noun "mishnah" is derived from a verb which means "to repeat." The verbatim repetition by a disciple of his master's views was not only a sign of appropriate respect for a man who could be compared to Moses, but was also the ordinary means by which these views were handed down from one generation to another. The "tanna" (the Aramaic word for "verbal repeater") was an important functionary in the rabbinic academy: a good tanna is compared to "a basket, full of books" (cf. b. Megillah 28b). Such men were the libraries of the academy, and a great deal hung on their ability and skill. This is why the insistence that "a man must speak in the words of his master" is so often expressed in rabbinic literature (cf. Bowker [1969] p. 49 n. 3 for citations), and why Mishnah itself declared in the name of R. Meir (second century A.D.), "Whoever forgets one word of his mishnah, scripture accounts it as if he had lost his soul" (Avoth 3:9). In Mishnah (capitalized to indicate the document, as distinct from the individual mishnayot [plural] it contains), a collection of rabbinic opinions probably compiled in the second century, the views of great masters are set out, largely from memory, in order to accomplish the threefold aim of ordering the Jewish community properly, ensuring the survival of rabbinic tradition, and preserving Torah (cf. Avoth 1:1). More will be said about the Mishnah (and the Talmud, its daughter) in the next paragraphs. For the moment we will simply say that Mishnah is both the most distinctive product of rabbinic thought and the foundation for its continuance.

Targum is the last genre to which we need to refer in the present context; the term refers to translations from the Bible into Aramaic. The inability of many Jews, even in Palestine, to speak Hebrew required that the scriptures be rendered in Aramaic in the course of worship in the synagogue, and such renderings also provided an occasion for the interpreter to introduce his own understanding of the text he was translating.

The Mishnah is, as it were, the constitution of rabbinic Judaism. It embodies the principle that the opinions of the rabbis are worth preserving and discussing, and that this entire process amounts to the continuing promulgation of Torah. When we speak of a "tanna" during the period in which the Mishnah took shape, we use a capital letter. We do so because we are referring to a particular group of men who were responsible for producing the Mishnah. Their importance within the history of Jewish religion would be difficult to exaggerate. Mishnah authorizes the sort of rabbinic discussion which is the central characteristic of post-biblical Jewish religion; in this sense the Tannaim (the plural form) invented Judaism. Jacob Neusner has rightly insisted on this point, and this sets him apart from those who accept the traditional teaching that the rabbis simply continued what Moses had started. What can be gathered of the development of rabbinic literature confirms his insight. There are references to the midrashic and targumic activities of rabbis in the second century and earlier, and individual midrashic and targumic interpretations are probably to be dated in this period (as is so, as we will see, in the case of the Isaiah Targum), but the authoritative scriptural exposition (called the "Great Midrash") and the standard Aramaic translations (Targum Onqelos to the Pentateuch, Targum Jonathan to the Prophets) were not officially recognized by the rabbis until Talmudic times. In contrast, the Mishnah as a whole is the very basis of the Talmud itself: Mishnah became an occasion for learned discussion within rabbinic academies, and some opinions were collected and appended to Mishnah forming the Talmud. Taken together, Mishnah and Talmud are unquestionably the best source for understanding the nature and development of rabbinic thought.

Before proceeding further, an example passage from Mishnah, with supplemental material in Talmud, should be described to the reader, so that the character of the literature can be experienced. Mishnah is divided into six "orders," of which the second is called "Festival" (Mo'ed); here one finds such subjects treated of as the sabbath, the definition of a sabbath's journey (going beyond which would break the prohibition of work in Exodus 20:10), the preparation of Passover lambs, payment of the Temple tax, the celebration of the Day of Atonement, of Tabernacles, of festivals in general, of New Year, fasting, how the book of Esther is to be read in the feast of Purim, work which could be performed between major feast days, the requirements placed on Jews for the observance of festivals. The "order" is not discursively presented, but "Festival" serves as a general category under which material is gathered, and some of the discussions included here fit uneasily into even this rather broadly construed context.

Each order is, in turn, subdivided into tractates, which serve further to categorize the material presented; the tractate called "Scroll" (Megillah) in the order "Festival" deals, for example, with the scroll of Esther as read during Purim (a term which means "lots," as was applied, for reasons unknown, to the feast celebrating the events recounted in Esther). It is customary to refer to a passage in Mishnah by tractate, not order, and to specify the reference further by chapter and paragraph. Capital or lower case "m" is sometimes prefixed to the name of the tractate in order clearly to show that the reference is to Mishnah, not Talmud.

We will consider Megillah 3:3, which deals with the use which may or may not be made of a ruined synagogue. The very subject matter again demonstrates that Mishnah is not systematically laid out. However, before the reader concludes that this material is irrelevant to the main topic, he might consider that the book of Esther is very much concerned with the persecution of Jews, which is the circumstance in which a synagogue might be ruined. The format of Mishnah is neither discursive, nor designed for elementary education; its very structure is a challenge to associative thinking and reflection. This structure reflects the purpose of discussion in rabbinic academies, which was to develop and refine a view of individual and communal life under Torah, not — in the first instance — to produce a manual of practice which any Jew could easily assimilate and follow.

The rabbis' discussions often resulted in the commendation or rejection of certain beliefs and practices, but Mishnah is designed more to arrive at these conclusions than to communicate them to the public. A failure to appreciate the genre of rabbinic literature has in the past contributed to the hasty condemnation of the whole of Judaism as "legalistic." Mishnah Megillah 3:3 deals, then, with the question of what to do when a synagogue has been ruined. In the name of R. Judah, probably Judah ben (or "son of") Ilai, a second century rabbi, the assertion is made that the site is not an appropriate place for funeral laments, or for work which might require a large open space, or for use as a short cut. A scriptural justification is then provided: Leviticus 26:31 has God promise that, if the people of Israel do not walk in his ways, "I will desolate your sanctuaries." This is taken to imply that, even in their desolation, such sites are still sanctuaries and should not be used for profit. Megillah 3:3 concludes by prescribing that even the grass that grows in a ruined synagogue should not be picked.

The wars of 63-70 and c. 132-135 A.D., in which Rome twice crushed attempts to re-establish an autonomous Jewish nation, left immense devastation in and around Palestine, and synagogues had been a particular target both for military campaigners and violent Gentile mobs. R. Judah was not dealing with an abstrusely theoretical or unusual event, but with an all too pressing reality: what should Jews do with demolished synagogues, which it might be impossible to rebuild for economic or political reasons, but which could be exploited to the advantage of the community? What did Torah say? As written, Torah said nothing, but as expounded by R. Judah, it offered guidance.

In Talmud, the passage from Mishnah we have just described is reproduced, and comments from other rabbis are appended. In the name of "our rabbis" — that is (probably), teachers from an ancient period before specific names were attached to opinions — synagogues are said not to be suitable places for eating, drinking, strolling, taking shelter from heat and rain, or for private funeral speeches. All such activities would bring a synagogue into disrepute. The proper use of a synagogue is that of reading the scripture, repeating mishnah and delivering public funeral speeches. This, then, is said to be the general attitude which underlies R. Judah's particular view in regard to ruined synagogues. Talmud can be seen at times to provide the context within which the passage from Mishnah at issue can more readily be understood.

Most of this discussion occurs on a single page of Talmud, in the tractate also called Megillah (the first few lines are on the preceding page). Talmud is referred to by the name of the tractate in question (as in the case of Mishnah, but sometimes with a "b" or "B" prefixed, to indicate the official, Babylonian Talmud) and by folio, not by chapter and paragraph. The page numbers are as assigned in the edition of Daniel Bomberg of Venice in the sixteenth century, with "a" designating the front, and "b" the back, of the page. The single page we are considering provides much more than a context for R. Judah's opinion; the thought behind his mishnah is elucidated by other rabbis so as to address conditions and circumstances which Judah himself did not have in mind. A rabbi named Assi (who lived during the third and fourth centuries A.D.) poses the question, for example, of Babylonian synagogues: some of these were built with the stipulation that they might be used for certain designated non-religious purposes. The upshot of the discussion which follows is that this should not be used as a pretext to use the synagogue for purposes which were not originally stipulated.

The discussion so far described in Megillah 28b all treats of "halakhah," that is, prescriptive teaching laying down what behaviour is proper. In addition to halakhah, Talmud (in common with rabbinic literature generally) also presents "haggadoth" (singular: haggadah), or illustrative stories which express principles in narrative rather than prescriptive form. In Megillah 28b, a haggadah is told which relates that one day three rabbis were discoursing in the open air when a shower started. They took refuge in a synagogue, not — they said — for shelter, but because there should be clarity in the discussion of Torah, which the rain was interfering with. Unsympathetically viewed, this haggadah instances a casuistical attitude. It would perhaps be fairer to say that the rabbis, in telling such stories, conveyed their awareness that the halakhoth (the plural of halakhah) they transmitted were not unbending legal regulations, but gave guidance which was to be taken seriously, but not so litera-listically that they got in the way of the style of life they were supposed to promote. This haggadah leads on, by a process akin to free association, to a discussion of how one should behave if one's discussion of Torah in a synagogue is inter-rupted by being called out to attend to some other business; basically, the advice given is that one should finish the thought at hand (whether one is an advanced student or a child just beginning to learn scripture by heart), and then get up to leave. The Talmudic discussion then returns to the wording in Mishnah, asking what is meant by a public funeral speech. In what follows, this question is answered by a series of haggadoth in which examples of rabbinic partici-pation in funerals are given; the implication is that rabbinic involvement is required to make a funeral "public." The stories, however, are also presented for their own sake, to illustrate the value of assiduously learning and discussing halakhah.

In this one passage of Talmud, one can see illustrated the extraordinary richness of the literature as a whole which drove one great modern teacher, J. H. Hertz, to use vivid imagery in order to convey his long-standing impression of it. Using a traditional metaphor of Talmud as an ocean, he speaks of its depth and size, its mysterious currents, and its variety of storm and calm (1935, p. xxvi). As Hertz goes on to say, this is not a book which is to be understood without the aid of a skilled guide, and one of the distinctive marks of Judaism throughout its history has been a consistent emphasis on offering guidance in the exposition of Mishnah and Talmud. Indeed, the relationship between Mishnah and Talmud provides the paradigm example of how exposition, in the rabbinic understanding, should be carried out. These great collections are designed for experts, as they were compiled by experts. They evidence the academic prowess of intramural rabbinic discussion such as took place in the academies of the learned.

An appreciation of the nature of rabbinic literature necessarily involves the recognition that we cannot read in Mishnah, Talmud, Midrash and Targum — taken at face value —about Judaism in the time of Jesus. On the whole, these documents, which constitute the foundation of rabbinic Judaism, represent a later and more specialized religious ethos than that in which Jesus operated. This orientation to Rabbinica is to be contrasted to that of Geza Vermes, who undertakes — largely on the basis of rabbinic sources — to reconstruct the historical context in which Jesus preached. How John's Gospel can be called relatively "remote" from the time and theology of Jesus (1973, p. 16) in the same book in which rabbinic documents from a very much later period are used to describe "first-century Judaism" (p. 9) and even the Galilee of Jesus' day (pp. 52ff.) is not explained. Indeed, Vermes appears to approximate the traditional notion of the rabbis that Judaism progressed in an unbroken line of succession from Moses.

Jewish documents from the first century and earlier present a very different picture. A few examples will perhaps suffice to illustrate this point. The famous discoveries at Qumran evidence a style of biblical interpretation quite unlike the rabbis', a peculiarly antagonistic view of contemporary worship in the Temple, and a hierarchical structure manifestly dissimilar to that described or presupposed in Mishnah. Books such as *4 Ezra* and *2 Baruch* show us that some Jews — in a distinctly non-rabbinic manner — actually produced literary works in the names of prominent biblical figures which purported to depict the events leading up to God's final intervention in history. The first century Jewish historian Josephus describes generally three groups of Jews (Essenes, Sadducees and Pharisees), which he likens to philosophical schools (*Jewish Wars* II:8 and *Antiquities* XVIII:8), and he contrasts their teachings on such fundamental matters as the place of fate in Israel's faith. As if this picture of diversity were not sufficiently complex, Josephus refers to all three groups in this context in order to insist that a certain revolutionary, Judas the Galilean, belonged to none of them. The early Judaism of Jesus' time seems to have been so heterogeneous that to claim his continuity or discontinuity with the religion of his day in general terms is problematic in the extreme: in almost anything he did or said, he would have been accepted by some Jews and rejected by others.

The rabbis, however, did not invent Judaism *de novo*. Methodologically, they were traditionalists who handed on the views of predecessors. This process, indeed, occasioned their interpretation as they applied old and revered principles to new situations. We have already observed that rabbinic literature might give us an insight into Jesus' occupation of the Temple, and such instances of correspondence between Rabbinica and the New Testament suggest that the former reflect at least something of Jewish religious life in the first century A.D. Perhaps the most famous instance of such correspondence is the teaching of love for one's neighbour as the key to the law, which is to some extent common to Hillel and Jesus. In Shabbath 31a, a heathen is said to come to Shammai (Hillel's contemporary and major competitor) asking to be taught the whole of Torah while the would-be proselyte stood on one foot (that is, in a very brief time). Shammai, true to his character as it is reflected in Rabbinica, repulsed the man with a measuring rod. Undaunted, the Gentile put the same proposal to Hillel, who said, "What is hateful to you, do not do to your neighbour: that is the whole Torah, while the rest is commentary thereon. Go and learn it." There is no question of an exact identity between this story and Matthew 7:12 (its nearest parallel in the New Testament), but that a kindred attitude is brought to expression in the two passages is obvious, as was discussed long ago by G. F. Moore (1927[2], pp. 86-88). Nonetheless, recent books on the relationship between Jesus and the Jewish religion of his day, such as that by John Riches (1980, p. 131), can refer to Matthew 7:12 as if it were altogether startling in a Jewish context without even citing Shabbath 31a.

Moore also refers to a number of stories about Hanina

ben Dosa, another contemporary of Jesus who was a notable healer (1927[1], pp. 377-378; cf. A. Büchler [1922] pp. 81-102). Several of these are also mentioned by Geza Vermes (1973, pp. 72-78), who unfortunately omits to cite Moore's classic work. Perhaps the Ḥanina story most conspicuously similar to one told of Jesus (cf. John 4:46-53; Matthew 8:5-13; Luke 7:1-10) is given in Berakhot 34b. It is there related that Rabbi Gamaliel's son fell ill, and he sent two emissaries to Ḥanina with the request that he pray for the child. Ḥanina prayed in an upper room, came down, and told the emissaries the fever had departed. They asked Ḥanina whether he were a prophet. He replied most emphatically that he was not, but that experience had taught him that when his prayer came easily, it was accepted. The emissaries noted the hour in writing and returned to Gamaliel, who told them that at just the time they had noted the fever had subsided and his son had asked for water.

Rabbinica abounds with material which is comparable with passages in the New Testament. Readily available compendia set out such evidence in a way which permits the reader to consider it; the work of Paul Billerbeck (1924-1928) must be mentioned in this regard. Of course, when using compendia of this kind, one can easily form misimpressions about rabbinic teaching: passages are cited only briefly, and recourse to an edition of the work in question is necessary to put readings in context. Then, too, Billerbeck — along with many scholars in his time — conceived of Judaism as a legalistic religion, and his judgment does seem to have influenced his selection of the evidence. In a recent volume, entitled *Paul and Palestinian Judaism* (1977), E. P. Sanders argues cogently that we should understand law in Judaism, not as a means of earning God's favour, but as a way of remaining within the covenant graciously bestowed by God on Israel. Accordingly, he calls in question the basis on which Billerbeck worked, and rightly argues that this unrivalled handbook should be used as a means of access to Rabinnica, not as a replacement for reading it (pp. 42ff.).

Neither Sanders's criticisms nor others to a similar effect, however, has vitiated the essential insight which Billerbeck's monumental volumes so authoritatively convey: the Judaism of the rabbis is comparable to a great deal in the New Testament, especially when we set Jesus' teaching and ministry alongside the views and actions attributed to first century rabbis. This insight, and its substantial affirmation by Billerbeck, is what underlies contributions such as that by Geza Vermes (1973). Neusner's strictures in respect of Mishnah as a basically specialist and, from the point of view of New Testament studies, late source are crucially important, however, since without them the student can be led into an anachronistic reading of the evidence. But we would be pressing Neusner's critique to the point of ignoring the evidence to hand were we to deny the degree of similarity and continuity which Billerbeck, Moore, Vermes and others have shown to exist between the New Testament and Rabbinica.

The New Testament itself is also a vital source for understanding the development of Judaism: the earliest description of Palestinian synagogue practice, for example, is presented in the fourth chapter of Luke's Gospel. Not until the end of the first century (according to Berakhoth 28b), by which time the bulk of the New Testament had achieved a form which we would easily identify with the documents as we know them, was a clause added to the standard daily prayer (called the Eighteen Benedictions) which called down destruction on the *"Noṣᵉrīm"* (that is, the followers of the Nazarene; cf. Moore [1927[1]] p. 292). It has recently been argued by Reuven Kimelman (1981) that the wording of the curse text is directed against a small Jewish Christian sect from a later period. His argument is cogent in respect of the wording, but it does not explain why the curse itself is so prominent and appears so early; the understanding that early followers of Jesus were the target group provides an explanation. Of course, no disciple of Jesus could have participated in the liturgy of a synagogue in which such a form of prayer was used, and insofar as the innovation instituted by the rabbis at Yavneh was accepted, the mission to the synagogue, so prominent earlier in the century (as

Acts attests), must effectively have been stifled. Although it no doubt was born of the growing tension between the two groups (which the New Testament also reflects at many points), this official move was decisive both for Judaism and the Church. For the former it implied the programmatic rejection of Christian claims in the exposition of Torah; for the latter, already a largely Gentile movement, it meant that the umbrella of Judaism, under which shelter could be taken to avoid the requirement to participate in the imperial cult, was removed, and persecution by the Romans was not long to be delayed. Of these events, however, neither Jesus nor his followers before the last quarter of the first century had to take account; for them the notion of a Church independent of the synagogue would have seemed as odd as that of a synagogue in which the claims of Jesus could not be discussed.

The continuity between the New Testament and Rabbinica teaches us that the Judaism of the rabbis was far from substantively innovative. Just as they claimed, they did reach back to the views of teachers in the period before 70 in order to seek guidance in interpreting Torah. They were faithful, as well as ardent, traditionalists. For this reason, we may call the Jewish religion of Jesus' time "early Judaism." Early Judaism was more varied than rabbinic Judaism, as we have mentioned, and teachers in this period did not enjoy the status rabbis later possessed, and all the training and collegial support which the academies were one day to provide. Teachers such as Jesus, although called "rabbi" as a matter of course (Matthew 26:25, 49; Mark 9:5; 10:51; 11:21; 14:45; John 1:38, 49; 3:2; 4:31; 6:25; 9:2; 11:8, and cf. the reference to John the Baptist in 3:26), employed arguments from scripture which do not follow the more developed pattern of their later, more academic counterparts. (Cf. D. M. Cohn-Sherbock [1979] and [1981], who anachronistically claims that this evidences Jesus' departure from the rabbinic norms of his day.) Yet the manifest continuity of these early teachers with the professional rabbis of the post-Yavneh period justifies the claim that their teaching was a foundational contribution to the compilation of Rabbinica and therefore to the emergence of Judaism proper after the dreadful events of 70 A.D.

2. *Targum Research and Early Judaism*

We know, then, that Jesus taught in the milieu of early Judaism, and therefore — unless there is hard evidence to the contrary — that he employed religious language from this milieu which would have been familiar to the various and non-expert Jewish audiences he primarily addressed. What we lack, however, is direct access to the sort of language and concepts that Jesus' hearers were accustomed to. No doubt, first century sectarian writings and the Pseudepigrapha (some of which are mentioned above) indirectly reflect the common religiosity of their day, but on the whole such documents better evidence the beliefs of distinctive groups within early Judaism than those of the generality of Jews living in Palestine at the time. That we need to inform ourselves as to the views of a broad consensus of Jews in the period is evident, because the Gospels and Acts make it quite clear that Jesus and his followers did not restrict their preaching to any single group or collection of groups within early Judaism as a whole, nor to an expert rabbinic circle. This is the impression also given by the first century Roman historian Tacitus, who refers to Christianity as a "mischievous superstition" which broke out in Judea generally and later infected Rome itself (*Annals* 15:44). Writers such as Tacitus may not rely on sources other than the New Testament, but, at the least, they show us how responsible historians of the period evaluated the New Testament from their own critical points of view. That these sources powerfully suggest there was a widely admitted historical aspect in the preaching of the early Church seems obvious, and the implications of this general observation will be explored more fully in the introduction to part two ("Jesus and the Targum to Isaiah"). What is particularly interesting in respect of the present concern is that, in order to appreciate Jesus' message, we must come to an understanding of early Judaism which is based more broadly than on the impressions we might gather from the sectarian and pseudepigraphical writings.

In recent years, the Scandinavian scholar Birger Gerhardsson has argued in several volumes that the Twelve orally preserved and handed on sayings of and stories about Jesus in the manner of rabbis in their academies and therefore that the Synoptic Gospels present us substantively with words of Jesus which derive from the trained minds of those who were associated with him in his ministry (1979, p. 90). As this is the most radical form of the argument that there is an analogy between rabbinic literature and the New Testament, its logic and evidential basis need to be evaluated. For the analogy even to be possible, rabbinic literature after 70 A.D. must be taken to typify rabbinic discussion before 70. Such a supposition is, as we have already seen, seriously to be questioned (cf. especially M. Smith [1963]). Rabbinic documents — and the materials contained in them — must be dated rigorously before they are used to characterize early Judaism in the time of Jesus. Moreover, we have already remarked that rabbinic literature is the child of intramural rabbinic discussion; the Gospels, even as read among those already baptised, were not intended to serve essentially academic interests. In a word, Gerhardsson has shown neither that what the rabbis said after 70 corresponded to what their predecessors said before 70 (or to the way in which the early dicta were handed on), nor that it would have mattered greatly to the generality of Jews living in the earlier period to know that a rabbi of the time took a given position.

Further, Gerhardsson's thesis, although not to the extent of Michael Goulder's (who urges us [1974 and 1978] to see the Gospels as examples of midrash), depends on establishing a kinship between the Gospels and some genre, or combination of genres, of Jewish literature. But the Gospels are not Mishnah or Talmud, where the views and attitudes of various sages are brought together so as to illuminate the various issues under discussion; in the Gospels there is but one rabbi that matters, and he himself is the only basic issue.

The Gospels are not Midrash, where the attempt is made systematically to relate the sayings and doings of different rabbis to a biblical text; in the Gospels the "text" is Jesus, and the Bible is cited to illuminate his words and deeds, rather than the reverse. The Gospels are not Targums, where the interpretation of biblical passages from Hebrew into Aramaic is designed to help the reader or hearer to a correct and vivid understanding of the passage in question; the Gospels present translations of biblical texts only incidentally, and expound Jesus' life, death and resurrection, not a pericope or series of pericopae.

Elements in the Gospels might, under comparative analysis, be shown to be mishnaic, midrashic or targumic, and this may be taken as evidence of the sorts of methods Jesus and his followers used to convey their teachings, and of the milieu in which they operated. But such analysis, in that it can only concern individual passages or strata in the Gospels, must acknowledge from the outset that the texts of the Gospels as we have them are not essentially like any ancient Jewish document. Our Gospels can only be classed as mishnah or midrash or targum if those categories are stretched so far beyond the description of actual examples of Jewish literature that they cease being literary categories at all. Finally, every student of rabbinic literature knows that the rabbis generally cannot be described as historians, so that to speak of the general reliability or authenticity of the Gospels on the basis of their similarity to Rabbinica is, to say the least, questionable. We read in one Talmudic passage that a certain rabbi said something, only to find the same saying ascribed to another rabbi elsewhere; rabbis who lived in different centuries are commonly presented as partners in dialogue; heavenly voices, appearances of Elijah, healings, exorcisms, miracles outside the usual experience of nature and other prodigies are associated with several rabbis; at one point Jesus himself is portrayed as executed by stoning (Sanhedrin 43a). It remains to be seen whether Rabbinica is a sound basis on which to understand pre-70 Jewish teachers, whether the New Testament is essentially like any combination of known Jewish teaching genres, and whether a positive response to the first two suggestions tells us anything in the end about the historicity of the Gospels.

Within the context of this discussion, recent investigation of the Targums is significant for two reasons: (1) because the Targums were designed to be used in synagogue worship, it has been held that they better represent popular piety than Intertestamental literature and Rabbinica, and (2) a strong case has been made for the pre-Christian origin of certain extant Targums. If both these assertions were true, the Targums would then be seen as the most important documents available for understanding the milieu in which Jesus and his first followers preached. The argument for both contentions is set out vigorously and carefully in two major contributions from Martin McNamara (1966, 1972), but the ensuing debate has also been vigorous, so that some description of the nature and date of the Targums must be offered here.

The very language of the Targums reflects the purpose for which they were developed. The use of Aramaic in Palestine was an inheritance from the establishment of Persian hegemony in the sixth century B.C., and the use of the language as a *lingua franca* survived the demise of the empire, and the subsequent ebb and flow of Ptolemaic, Seleucid, Hasmonaean and Roman hegemony. By the first century A.D., Aramaic seems to have been the primary language in multi-lingual Palestine. To some degree, of course, Hebrew continued to be used, at least in certain circles, as the Qumran finds have confirmed beyond a doubt. Greek especially — as the language of Mediterranean commerce and culture — was known to an extent, and Latin also came into the picture with the Roman military and civic presence. On the strength of his painstaking analysis of documentary and inscriptional evidence relating to the languages used in this politically troubled region in the time of Jesus, however, Joseph A. Fitzmyer (1970 and 1979) has demonstrated the predominance of Aramaic as the popular language. Moreover, the Greek New Testament itself actually presents some Aramaic phrases (in transliteration) which Jesus used (cf. especially his last words, as given in

Matthew 27:46 and Mark 15:34), and frequently employs diction which seems less a reflection of commonly spoken Greek than of translation from Aramaic into Greek (cf. Black [1967] and Zimmermann [1979]). Although Jesus and his first followers, along with their contemporaries, may possibly have used other languages as well, Aramaic was what they used in their daily speech.

In the regular worship in synagogues, where the reading of scripture constituted the heart of the service, the Hebrew Bible was simply too unfamiliar in its language, and often too obscure in its imagery, to be left untranslated. Of course, the danger had to be dealt with that there might be a confusion in people's minds between the actual written text of scripture and the often highly paraphrastic renderings of the Targums. (As is consistent with our usage of such terms as "mishnah," "midrash" and "talmud" and their derivatives, we only capitalize the "t" in "Targum" when actual, extant documents are in question.) The rabbis therefore set down precise instructions for the interpreter (meturgeman) who delivered a targum (Megillah 32a): the targum was not to be spoken before the biblical (that is, Hebrew) text had been read aloud in its own, holy language, and the reader of the text — even if he knew the passage appointed by heart —had to keep his eyes on the open scroll, to show that the written text, and none other, was being delivered. After the scroll was closed, the meturgeman rose to speak, facing the congregation with his eyes necessarily averted from the sacred text. He gave an interpretation, not the written word, and his actions had to attest that fact. These interpretations were popular: they were in a familiar language, and they often put puzzling figures of speech, which are difficult to understand even when they are translated, into more easily understood forms. As we can see in the Targums that have come down to us, the meturgeman also had the freedom to append sentences, and even complete stories, to his rendering, by way of interpretation. The rabbis were wary of permitting too much liberty to be taken, but they allowed —in some instances — for more than one paraphrase of a single passage to be given. Their reason for allowing such freedom was simple and pastoral: "Since the people like it, they pay attention and hear" (Megillah 21b). Some translations were so much a possession of folk usage and memory that rabbis, we are told, consulted with speakers of Aramaic on occasion to recover the most suitable phrasing in their targumic versions (Midrash Rabbah [Genesis 79]). The Targums are therefore a species of interpretative literature, and the outcome of a dialectical relationship between folk religiosity and rabbinic discussion.

The dating of Targums has been a contentious matter, to a certain extent because rabbinic literature is curiously confusing in this regard. The Isaiah Targum, for instance (along with the other Targums to the Prophetic books), is ascribed to a disciple of Hillel named Jonathan ben Uzziel, but he is said to be a follower of the biblical prophets Haggai, Zechariah and Malachi (Megillah 3a). Our confusion is compounded when renderings of Prophetic passages which are clearly related to those of the Targum ascribed to Jonathan are transmitted in the name of Joseph bar Ḥiyya, a fourth century sage of the Babylonian academy at Pumbedita (cf., for example, Targum Isaiah 5:17 and Pesahim 68a, and, for further evidence, Chilton [1982] pp. 2-3, 120). How are we to make sense of such assertions? We cannot do so by treating them as if Talmud were claiming that Jonathan or Joseph was the exclusive author of the Targum. Indeed, as soon as we use the term "author," we are perhaps misleading ourselves, in that it does not convey anything of the extensive, dialectical interaction between synagogue and academy which we have seen to lie behind the Targums. The Talmudic passages cited show how the rabbis' awareness of this extensive process was illustrated by them in haggadah: Jonathan is an important figure in the origin of the material included in the Isaiah Targum, but the contribution of Joseph centuries later is also to be reckoned with. The assertion that Jonathan was a follower of the biblical prophets is probably best taken as expressing, not the chronology of Jonathan, but the respect in which his work, as a continuation of that of the prophets, was held.

The place of the rabbis, over an extended period of time,

in the development of the Targums is an easily established fact, and it is obvious in any case that the evolution of synagogue practice alone cannot explain the existence of written, authoritative Targums. The usage of centuries presumably produced a measure of commonality in the interpretations spoken in synagogue, but the step from rendering those passages which happen to have been read publicly to translating an entire book or series of books was a considerable one. Some variety in interpretation was countenanced by the rabbis, as we have seen, but their attitude was not one of *laissez-faire*. How scripture is translated can crucially influence the formation of a people's faith, and the rabbis were sensitive to the dangers of sloppy or ill-considered renderings. Exodus 24:10 posed special difficulties, for example, because the Hebrew text there reads, "and they (that is, Moses with Aaron, Nadab, Abihu and the seventy elders) saw the God of Israel." How can that be, when in the same book God says to Moses, "man will not see me and live" (33:20)? If one were to translate Exodus 24:10 word for word, people might be misled into thinking God is easily visible to men, and so some interpreters rendered the passage, "and they saw the angel of the God of Israel." The difficulty with this solution, however, is that it derogates the manifestation of God spoken of in the biblical text into a merely angelic appearance. In his famous, at first sight paradoxical, dictum, R. Judah ben Ilai rejected both a literalistic and a too paraphrastic rendering of this verse:

> If one translates a verse literally, he is a liar; if he adds thereto, he is a blasphemer and a libeller (Kiddushin 49a)

In the same Talmudic passage, the Pentateuch Targum called Onqelos (after the second century proselyte who was largely responsible for it) is approvingly cited because it solves the dilemma any translator might find himself in who takes R. Judah's words seriously. This Targum renders Exodus 24:10 as, "and they saw the glory of the God of Israel." "Glory" is not an addition in the sense that "angel" is, because God is not replaced by another figure; at the same time, the impression is not given that God is visible to men. Moreover, "glory" is precisely what Moses asks to see, and does see, later in Exodus (33:18, 22-23), so that the translation in Onqelos can also be said to contribute to an understanding of scripture which is consistent from one passage to another. In this apparently technical discussion, therefore, the rabbis showed that their concern for appropriate translation in the synagogue was more than a matter of exercising their resourcefulness, but was also grounded in their awareness that careless translation can only lead to distorted faith.

Although the rabbis sought to ensure the orthodoxy of the Targums used in synagogue worship, they were not always successful in doing so. The Targums, even in their extant, generally late manuscripts, sometimes preserve renderings which were explicitly forbidden by the rabbis, and even interpretations of passages the rabbis said should not be translated at all. The Pentateuch Targum called Pseudo-Jonathan at Leviticus 18:21 renders "and you will not give your seed to pass over to Moloch" as referring to sexual intercourse with Gentiles: such an interpretation is proscribed in Megillah 4:9, and in fact Onqelos honours the proscription by offering a more literal translation. But Onqelos, along with most of the printed Pentateuch Targums, seemingly contradicts Megillah 4:10 in presenting an interpretation of the shameful episode of Reuben taking his father's concubine (Genesis 35:22), which Mishnah clearly states "is to be read out but not interpreted." (These two examples are taken from Martin McNamara [1966], pp. 46-51). Such divergences of the Targums from rabbinic strictures have been taken as evidence that the Targums essentially antedate the rabbinic regulations (cf. Alejandro Díez Macho [1973] and the more qualified position of McNamara [1966 and 1972]). Although frequently employed, this argument simply fails to do justice to the complexity of the data it adduces (cf. A. D. York [1974]). Since the Targums do not consistently contradict mishnaic regulations, the divergences that have been identified might be taken to reflect, not the antiquity of the Targums, but the influence of variant popular or rabbinic traditions of uncertain dates (cf. Chilton [1980² and 1982]). These possibilities seem all the more likely when it is borne in mind that the very Targums which have been alleged to be early can be shown to have definite connections with classical rabbinic literature (cf. Davies and Chilton [1978] and Chilton [1980¹]).

Study of the language of the Targums has also been inconclusive in respect to their dates, although it has made possible a division of Targumic texts into linguistic categories. The Pentateuch Targum called Onqelos, authorized by the Babylonian Amoraim (rabbis who taught after the compilation of the Mishnah, and contributed to the Talmud), represents Babylonian Aramaic, while the Pentateuch Targum called Pseudo-Jonathan reflects a different, presumably Palestinian form of Aramaic such as is known from the Jerusalem Talmud. (Pseudo-Jonathan's language is similar to that of three other Pentateuch Targums which are also commonly classified as Palestinian: Neophyti I, the Cairo Geniza Fragments and the Fragment Targum). The Targum to the Prophets named after Jonathan appears to mediate between Babylonian and Palestinian Aramaic (Frankel [1872], Chilton [1982]). To summarize a complicated history of discussion (cf. Chilton [1980² and 1982]), the principal question has been whether Palestinian Aramaic is more ancient than the Babylonian dialect (so, for example, Díez Macho [1973]) or the reverse (so, for example, Joseph A. Fitzmyer [1971]). A major difficulty in deciding the question is posed by the date of the actual manuscripts to hand; they all come from periods long after the New Testament canon was fixed, and some are even medieval. The extent to which later copyists preserved the language of their exemplars without alteration is also open to question (cf. Raimundo Griñó [1977]). Nonetheless, the on-going analysis of the finds from the Qumran caves has tended to support Fitzmyer's position more than Díez Macho's (cf. Stephen A. Kaufman [1973]). Even so, it is obviously possible that the exegetical readings of any Targum might be more ancient than the language in which they happen to be expressed.

Martin MaNamara, whose books have already been cited, has shown that some Targumic passages, at any rate, seem to preserve understandings of the biblical text that are also expressed in the New Testament. In some cases, the agreement is so close, and so unlike the renderings of other ancient versions of the Old Testament, that it is best explained as the influence of Targumic tradition at some stage in the development of the New Testament. McNamara cites Luke 6:36, "Become merciful just as your Father is merciful," and describes its relationship to the rendering of Leviticus 22:28 in Pseudo-Jonathan, "My people, children of Israel, as our Father is merciful in heaven, so shall you be merciful on earth." The Hebrew text of this verse merely proscribes killing a cow or sheep on the same day as its young, without such a profound theological comment, so that the addition in the Targum is innovative beyond doubt, and its substantive agreement with Jesus' saying as handed down by Luke is so striking as to demand explanation (McNamara [1966] pp. 133-138). Although one may never exclude the general possibility that rabbinic documents, because they are more recent than the formation of the New Testament, may reflect (rather than underlie) Christian teaching, the present case can scarcely be considered one in which the rabbis have attempted to respond to a saying of Jesus. It is also quite unlikely that the Targums would take up an element from the Jesus tradition without qualification. Rather, McNamara seems to be right in citing this as an example of the dependence of the New Testament on a Targumic rendering. As he also points out, the enigmatic phrase, "the second death," which appears in Revelation 20:6, 14 is paralleled in Onqelos (Deuteronomy 33:6) and Jonathan (Isaiah 65:15ff.; cf. McNamara [1972] pp. 123f., 148).

To such examples of correspondence with the New Testament, possible parallels with the Qumran scrolls might be added. Naphtali Wieder pointed out long ago that the Targum to Habakkuk (1:16) and the famous Habakkuk Scroll agree in portraying idolatry in military terms, apparently with the standards of the Roman army in mind ([1953] p. 18). The observation of possible literary connections of this kind, however, cannot be applied to establish the antiquity of the Targums as we have them: any document might be more recent than the oldest material it contains. Then, too, one must be prepared to take account of the connections of the Targums with later literature. Samson H. Levey draws attention to Isaiah 11:4 in the Targum, where Rome is referred to under the cipher, known from her own mythology, "Romulus." Because this usage is not elsewhere evidenced until after the rabbinic period, Levey takes it as an indication that the entire Targum to the Prophets must be late ([1971] p. 194). The difficulty with this argument is that it assumes that the latest reading in the document determines the date of the whole, which is no more admissible than the assumption that the earliest reading is determinative. Later interpretations might well have been added to any Targum after it was completed in substance, and the fact that the Romulus reading is not included in all manuscripts of the Isaiah Targum inclines us to think that it is an example of a later insertion. The literary affinities of the Targums with other documents — including the New Testament — are therefore no basis on which to establish their dates absolutely, although they obviously help to suggest the general period during which the Targums took shape and were modified in the course of transmission.

Historical allusions which can be detected in the Targums do not provide us with an any more secure foundation for specifying the chronology of their evolution within the broad span of time suggested by the rabbinic haggadoth already mentioned. As Pinkhos Churgin observed in his classic monograph (1927), we find reference to the deplorable practices of priests in the Isaiah Targum, as if the Temple were still standing (28:1; pp. 23, 24) and in the same Targum an allusion to the resurgence and abuses of Babylonian power in the centuries after the destruction of the Temple (21:9; pp. 28, 29). Such allusions seem, then, to be as ambivalent as the literary connections and the language of the Targums.

Fundamentally, the same methodological difficulty attends all the attempts described to fix the date and provenience of the Targums, whether they proceed on the basis of parallels with other documents, historical allusions or our incomplete understanding of the development of the Aramaic language. All three procedures really only illuminate the provenience of that Targumic material which happens to be similar to a datable document, or which seems to presuppose a historical background known to us from other sources, or which is expressed in an idiom of Aramaic with which we are familiar. Clearly, investigations along these lines must be taken into account in any attempt to establish the origin of the Targums, but they have not yet explained the origin of the Targums as complete documents. In the final analysis, they cannot do so. Each Targum, because it provides us with a *continuous* paraphrase which attests the interpretative understandings of early Judaism and rabbinic Judaism, cannot be treated as a mere collection of individual traditions. Even when particular passages in the Targums can be characterized by the methods outlined, the results are not determinative of the theology, provenience and date of the complete Targums in which the passages appear. Practically speaking, the attempt to interpret the Targums comprehensively by means of these methods cannot succeed, because it is impossible to fix each verse in respect of historical allusions, literary connections or linguistic associations. A revised method needs to be developed and applied, which illuminates the Targums as complete works of extended, paraphrastic exegesis; this is the unique form and purpose they have within rabbinic literature.

The development of an analytic method which is suited to the nature of the Targums has been the major research interest of the present writer over the past several years, and I have applied such a method to a specific Targum in a volume entitled: *The Glory of Israel: The Theology and Provenience of the Isaiah Targum* (1982). The procedure begins simply with the isolation of terms and phrases which are so consistently repeated through the Targum as to suggest they are characteristic usages. The point is not what is earliest or latest in a Targum, but: what is so frequently used that it seems to reflect the concerns of the compiler who brought together earlier material, and whose work was supplemented by later additions? What motivated the collection of interpretative traditions into a continuous paraphrase? The characteristic usages provide us with the vocabulary to describe the theology of the Targum in its own terms, and can be considered against the historical background of the entire period during which the Targum took form, and compared with the New Testament and other early Jewish documents including Aramaic sources, and with rabbinic documents. By means of coordinating these findings with other methods in an analysis of the document itself, the provenience of the Targum as a composite whole is investigated, and indeed the method might be called composition criticism. (Obviously, the procedure owes a great deal to the redaction criticism of the New Testament, from which it differs in being less atomistic; cf. Chilton [1979]). The theological standpoint of the Targum, when it can be connected to datable documents, events or linguistic usages, also indicates its date as a composition.

The characteristic terms or phrases, then, manifest the exegetical framework of the Targum, which is its principal instrument of composition. The framework reflects the structure of the compiler's thought, his overall conception of the meaning of the book of Isaiah, in which he contexted the earlier traditions available to him, and on which later readings were hung. This compositional framework is therefore not to be taken as a straitjacket, to restrict all of the material included in the Targum to the date of its framework; the framework reflects the date of the theology and provenience of the compilation, not of the individual elements that were compiled (or later added). For this reason, analysis of the framework provides only a starting point for an evaluation of the various interpretations embodied in the Targum, and is no substitute for a step by step investigation of these constituent readings. Nonetheless, the method outlined does promise a means of appreciating the theological value of the Targum as a whole in its historical setting.

The exegetical framework of the Isaiah Targum is describable as a whole, but within the overall structure, distinctive tendencies are evident which reveal definite stages of development before the final framework emerged. The first major level of the framework was developed during the Tannaitic period, the formative era of rabbinic Judaism before the compilation of the Mishnah. At this stage the Temple service was a crucial issue, so that it is presupposed that the cult was still being carried out, or at least that it had not yet been definitively outlawed by the Romans. The second major level was developed during the Amoraic period, when the later rabbis undertook the further exposition of Judaism on the basis of the Mishnah, and when the simple facts of the destruction of the Temple and Israel's dispersal were accepted as part of the status quo. The framework in its final form, however, is the best point of departure, since the earlier stages of growth are only detectable as parts of its larger structure. The logic of this order of analysis also corresponds to the nature of the evidence to hand: the Targum as we know it, without certain date or attribution, is a literary entity, and we must understand its literary shape and structure before we can speak intelligently of the meaning, date or historical significance of the material it contains. Whenever the provenience of a document is uncertain, speculation in regard to its author and date should only be conducted on the basis of sound literary findings in respect of its purpose, message and genre. To reverse the order is to put our purely speculative notions ahead of solid documentary evidence.

The coordinated usage of diverse characteristic terms and phrases in the framework of the Isaiah Targum is focused on the restoration of the house of Israel, a restoration which implies return from the Diaspora to the land ordained by God for his people, and therefore also victory over the Gentile dominion which prevents this restoration. The following passages from the Isaiah Targum, especially when they are compared to the readings of the Hebrew text, illustrate this motif:

> 51.11: And the redeemed of the LORD will be gathered from their exiles, and they will enter into Zion with a song of praise, and eternal joy will be theirs, which does not cease, and a cloud of glory will cover their heads. They will find gladness and joy, and sorrow and sighing will desist from them, from the house of Israel.
> 51.9b: Have I not, congregation of Israel, shattered the mighty men for your sake, destroyed Pharaoh and his armies, which were strong as the dragon?

Comparison of these passages, which have been translated from the Aramaic editions of Sperber (1962) and Stenning (1949), with any competent rendering of the Hebrew text will also illustrate how dramatically the interpreters developed an innovative view of the meaning of the Isaian text. We are dealing here with a version of Isaiah which is substantially creative, even though it was offered as a translation of the Hebrew. At the same time, it should be stressed that the Targumic paraphrases are not usually arbitrary, but grow out of intelligent reflections on the meaning of the Hebrew text (cf. Koch [1972] and Chilton [1982] for examples).

Israel is promised, "You will be gathered with glory from the Lord" (58.8), and the interpreters' faith in the public manifestation of that glory which is in the end God's is unshakeable. The Temple and Jerusalem — where God's presence (Shekhinah) is said to dwell — are at the centre of the restoration, and the sanctuary is of extraordinary importance both as the source of the unique force which comes from God and as the goal of Israel's obedience. These two aspects of sanctuary usage can be illustrated with reference to a single passage (2.3):

> And many people will go and say, Come, and we will go up the mountain of the sanctuary house of the LORD,

the Shekhinah house of the God of Jacob, and he will teach us from the ways that are correct before him, and we will go in the teaching of his law, for from Zion the law will proceed, and the teaching of the word of the LORD from Jerusalem.

Obedience to the law as given on Sinai is the condition apart from which divine favour cannot be offered, just as rejection of the law occasions God's anger:

... they who have forsaken the law of the Lord will be destroyed (1.28).

God's word (Memra), however, remains constant in the election of Israel, whether this election is expressed in the favour which comes of obedience or in the wrath which comes of rebellion:

... by the word of the Lord of hosts this will be accomplished (9.6; v. 7 in the R.S.V.).

The same "word" (48:16c and cf. 40:13b) issues a summons to God's people through the prophets, as agents of his holy spirit, in order to appeal for repentance:

Who has ordered the holy spirit in the mouth of all the prophets, was it not the LORD? (40.13a)

The prophets appeal for righteousness from their people, righteousness akin to that of Abraham, for, while God is pictured as unmovable in his choice of Israel through Abraham, even when Israel rejects his own identity, Abraham is used as an example of the ethical course Israel is to follow. This comes to expression in the famous fifth chapter of Isaiah, where God's passionate and active concern for the righteousness of Israel is vividly portrayed:

The prophet said, I will now sing the praise of Israel,

who is like a vineyard, the seed of Abraham, my
friend...(5.1).

It is notable that the interpreters speak in the name of Isaiah
himself ("The prophet said...," cf. the Hebrew text) in
order to demand a repentance whose content is a return to
the law and proper Temple service:

> They were commanded to do the law, and they did not
> wish to do what they were commanded. The prophets
> prophesied to them that, if they repented, it would be
> forgiven them, and they did not accept the sayings of the
> prophets....They did not hope in the service of my
> sanctuary house...(28:10).

Repentance alone puts Israel in the position to receive the
vindication willed him by God. The purpose of the messiah
is precisely "...to subject many to the law"(53:11), because
such obedience occasions God's forgiveness and the restoration of Israel.

The principal and most striking feature of the framework
as a whole is its perennial relevance for Israel. The Tannaitic
and Amoraic interpreters agreed to a remarkable extent
precisely in regard to the place of Israel in the promises and
warnings voiced by Isaiah, and the Babylonian rabbis, evidently moved by the message of the framework, authorized
its transmission (Megillah 3a). Here is a message that pertains to all Israel, even when dispersed and disoriented,
without Temple and surviving on the sufferance of heathen
officials: he is called to hope in the rebuilding of the Temple
and the re-establishment of his autonomy. This Targum
constitutes both a consolation and a challenge to any form
of biblical faith which takes God's covenant with Israel
seriously, and it is particularly appropriate as such when
read within the context of the difficult circumstances which
surrounded and followed the destruction of the Temple.

The success of the Targum in its extant form as a contribution to the spiritual life of dispersed Israel makes it prob-

lematic to assign the entire framework to a single period. The usage of the same characteristic terms and phrases by interpreters from different times makes it difficult to determine where the work of one ends and that of another begins. The Targum frequently shares hopes and beliefs also reflected in the Eighteen Benedictions, the principal prayer of the entire rabbinic period, and this suggests that the rabbis might responsibly have used and approved such language in nearly any period between the dissolution of the Temple cult and the medieval attestation of the Targumic text.

The Targumic conception of the law as the means by which Israel draws near to God and realizes his very identity is reminiscent, for example, of the general movement of single-minded devotion to the law which began in the Maccabean period and reached its most lucid expression in rabbinic teaching. Nevertheless, the specific and emphatic connection between the law and the cult in the Targum, and the confidence that Israel, messianically restored, would establish itself with a teaching that originates from the Temple seems especially (although not exclusively) similar to the zealous, realistically articulated hope to the same effect expressed in Intertestamental literature (cf. 2:3, cited above, and *Sibylline Oracles* III. 710-723). This similarity is more obvious in respect of uses of the word "sanctuary," because, while the physical restoration of the Temple is a prominent expectation in the Targum, Intertestamental literature and among earlier rabbis, the Amoraic rabbis were far less eager to portray the rebuilding of the Temple in literal terms (cf. Targum Isaiah 24:16 and Kethuboth 112b). The usage of the Targum, therefore, would appear to reflect a Tannaitic framework within the document as a whole. Moreover, there is literary evidence within the document that two strata of the early framework should be distinguished, as a comparison of the following two passages will show:

Woe to him that. . . gives the turban to the wicked (priest)

of the sanctuary house of his praise...(28:1);
For the sanctuary house is desolate...(32:14).

In the first stratum, the restoration of the Temple is a matter
of reforming cultic service; the second presupposes that
actual rebuilding is necessary. The development of the Tannaitic framework before and after the destruction of the
Temple is therefore detectable.

In a contemporary work, the fifth book of the *Sibylline
Oracles*, we can see a similarly vehement hope in the concrete consolation of Jerusalem (cf. Collins [1974]). This
confidence is to be distinguished from the tendency of later
rabbinic exegesis, in which the consolation of Jerusalem is
seen more in her ethical righteousness than in political
reconstruction (cf. Berakhoth 10a). The Targumic description of Jerusalem (in both strata of the earlier framework)
reflects the oppression suffered under the Roman siege (cf.
8:8) and after its eventual success (cf. 54:1). Similarly, the
early framework shares with Intertestamental literature and
the Eighteen Benedictions the hope of a militarily triumphal
return from exile (cf. 51:9-11; the *Psalms of Solomon* 8: 28;
the tenth benediction in both the Babylonian and the Palestinian recensions). In contrast to the expectation of an
imminent return from the Diaspora, rabbis from the second
century and later developed a more accepting attitude to
exile, and portrayed God as banished with his people (cf.
Pesiqta Rabati 8:4). Within the earlier framework, exile is
initially (in the first stratum: cf. 8:18) a definite threat, and
then (in the second: cf. 57:17) a reality. All uses of the term
"Shekhinah" in the Targum presuppose a close identification of God's presence with the Temple (cf. 1:15), and consequently the Shekhinah is portrayed either as burdened by
cultic abuse (28:10) or as removed because of such abuse
(59:2). Among the later rabbis, the term came to be applied
much more generally to the divine presence with the individual, and also in various centres of rabbinic discussion (cf.
Leviticus Rabbah 11:7 and A. M. Goldberg [1969]). We
shall treat in part two of "the kingdom of God" in the

Targum; for the moment we may say simply that it appears concretely in strict association with Mount Zion, not — as in later sources — as an image of loyalty to the law.

Alongside the earlier framework, another can be discerned which echoes Amoraic motives. Here, sin in general, not specifically cultic abuses, is the reason for the Babylonian exile (cf. 43:14). The hope for a definitive end of the Babylonian tyranny is connected more with the penitence of the individual than with the repentance of Israel as a people (cf. 57:19). Because exile for the interpreters of the later framework is the situation in which one should cultivate right behaviour, the basic acceptance of this exile by the Amoraim as the status quo is presupposed (49:18). Moreover, Israel in the second framework is more a gathered community than a national "house": a postnationalistic perspective may here be detected (cf. 27:2). Nonetheless, the Amoraic interpreters did hold fast to much of the tradition that lay before them, as is evident, for example, in 48:15, 16. In this passage, we read the command to follow Abraham in respect of his vocation to cultic service, while in the Amoraic period it was far more fashionable to insist in connection with this verse that scholars should be accorded the respect owed to Moses (cf. Mo'ed Katan 16b). While the introductory phrase, "The prophet said," is generally used in the first framework to highlight statements that demand national repentance and express an imminent expectation of Jerusalem's vindication, in the second it is employed to emphasize the call for righteous individual behaviour in the face of the judgment that is to come (21:12). The Amoraic interpreters also extended the role of the messiah: in the second framework he is a presently existing witness of God's vindication (43:10), and not only, as in the first framework, he who, associated with a priestly colleague, enacts the law which proceeds from the Temple.

Although the two frameworks distinguish themselves from one another by their particular usages of characteristic words and phrases, their common work forms a complete exegetical scheme within which the traditional materials in the Targum procure their specific meaning. The theology of messianic vindication is a leading theme in both levels of the Targum, even if each level (and each stratum within the first level) has its own precise conception of what this vindication entails. The essential unity of the Targum, despite its rather complicated development, is underlined by the fact that some words — "holy spirit," "word" (Memra), and "glory" being good examples — are used indistinguishably in both frameworks. As the rings of a tree, which record the conditions of previous years, the two strata of the Tannaitic framework and the single, less extensive Amoraic framework attest the stages of the exegetical growth of the Targum to Isaiah.

The Targum as a whole, then, stands as a monument to the faith that God will redeem Israel. Its raw material was the tradition of synagogue interpretation, which the framework interpreters shaped according to their own acute understanding of the book of Isaiah and the theological tendencies of their times. Those times were far from easy, and it is remarkable that the earlier and more substantial level of the framework was developed precisely as Israel's national and cultic centre, the Temple, was threatened with — and then underwent — destruction. Harrowing circumstances were the occasion for a renewed expression of the certainty that God will act on behalf of his people, and whether we look at the vigorous nationalism of the Tannaitic framework interpreter, or at the more settled ethical teaching of the Amoraic framework interpreter, we are confronted in their joint work with the conviction that patient and thoughtful attention to the biblical text is what will lead Israel to the restored identity willed by God. Adversity and challenge were seen as an excuse neither for seeking refuge in past forms of piety, as if nothing had changed, nor for ignoring the traditions of the past, as if they offered no analogy to the trials of the present. They were rather seen as incentives to discover what it meant to be Israel, and to express that as clearly as possible. Quite apart from its possible relevance to the study of the New Testament, the Targum is valuable as an eloquent reminder that a vital, biblically based faith was the wellspring of early Judaism, and fed both primitive Christianity and rabbinic Judaism.

Part Two

JESUS AND THE
TARGUM TO ISAIAH

1. Initial Consideration

Our understanding of the development of the Isaiah Targum certainly does not permit us to assume that it was known to Jesus; even the earlier, Tannaitic framework only took shape a generation after his ministry. Relative to the formation of other rabbinic documents, however, this Targum is early, and is important for the insights it gives us into the theology and faith of early Judaism. Although the Targum as a thorough-going paraphrase of the book of Isaiah dates from periods after the death of Jesus, the conservative nature of its formation, in which traditions from the past were collected and handed on by the framework interpreters, suggests that some of the material available in the Targum represents the early Judaism in which Jesus himself believed, and which was the basis of his distinctive preaching.

The precise relationship, if there be any, which Jesus had with the Targumic material cannot be determined by assuming he had access to the Targum as we can read it today. Such a hypothesis would only beg the question. A critical approach to this question demands that we search for actual instances in which Jesus seems to have used Targumic material. My own interest in the Targum was aroused in 1974, when I began research on Jesus' announcement of the kingdom of God. That study, completed in 1976 and published in 1979, in the first place submitted the announcement sayings to a redaction critical treatment: the particular interpretation of a saying by the individual Evangelist was analyzed. As they handed on sayings, the Evangelists placed them in certain contexts, sometimes adjusted their wording so as to make the meaning clearer, and associated them with those themes that are most prominent in their respective Gospels. The Gospel writers were editors or redactors of the Jesus tradition which was given to them, and they shaped the form in which we know it. The purpose of the earlier study, however, was not merely to determine how these editors shaped the sayings, but also thereby to define the traditional elements in them which must have been passed on to the Evangelists by their predecessors (cf. Luke 1:2). At this point, the study became tradition critical: the attempt was made to determine whence these traditions derived by comparing them to other ancient literary sources. (The reviews by Stanton [1980] and Tuckett [1980] fail to refer to this clearly stated principle in *God in Strength*; cf. p. 67 in particular.) The specific, linguistic connections between Jesus' kingdom announcement and the Targum are set out in that study. The present purpose is to compare the Targumic conception of the kingdom with that of Jesus in order to introduce the question of Jesus' relation to the Isaiah Targum.

The theology of the Tannaitic framework has been described in part one; the phrase "kingdom of God" or "kingdom of the LORD" is used in a way which suits the belief in the imminent vindication of Israel. Consistently, the revelation of God's rule is spoken of in close connection with Mount Zion. The first usage occurs in Isaiah 24:23, and the logic of the Targumic rendering is immediately clear when it is compared to the Hebrew (Masoretic) text:

MT: because the Lord of hosts reigns on Mount Zion

> **Tg:** because the kingdom of the Lord of hosts will be revealed on Mount Zion.

The use of the verb "to reign" (*mlk*) obviously justifies the mention of "the kingdom" (*mlkwt'*). Immediately after this passage, the Targum (along with the Hebrew text) portrays with vivid imagery the feast for all nations (25:6-8). The association of the kingdom with a festal image is reminiscent of Jesus' promise in Matthew 8:11 (cf. Luke 13:28, 29) that many will come from outside Israel and celebrate table fellowship with Abraham, Isaac and Jacob in the kingdom. Nonetheless, it must be borne in mind that the festal imagery in the Targum at Isaiah 25:6-8 includes reference to the punishment of the nations, which is not part of Jesus' announcement. From the beginning, then, we can discern an exclusivist tendency in the Targum which distinguishes it from the theology of Jesus.

The close connection between the kingdom and Zion is also evident in 31:4:

> **MT:** the LORD of hosts will descend to fight upon Mount Zion
> **Tg:** so the kingdom of the LORD of hosts will be revealed to dwell upon Mount Zion.

Contextually, the connection is also apparent in 40:9 and 52:7 (cf. the introduction in each case):

> **MT:** behold your God
> **Tg:** the kingdom of your God is revealed
> **MT:** your God reigns
> **Tg:** the kingdom of your God is revealed.

In addition to its pertinence to his theology of messianic vindication, the interpreter's kingdom language is also striking in other respects. Firstly, the term "to reign" is not present in the corresponding Hebrew text in two cases (31:4 and 40:9), so that "the kingdom" cannot be said to be presented as a mere noun substitute for a verb. Rather, it is

God's personal and dynamic intervention on behalf of his people which is at issue in these usages, and indeed in all four passages. The term "kingdom" therefore refers to God's active power or strength, and not merely to his theoretical kingship. Secondly, the kingdom is something that is to be "revealed," which implies — according to rabbinic usage (cf. Dalman [1902] p. 97 and Moore [1927] p. 374) —that the kingdom is a reality which awaits disclosure. Thirdly, the kingdom in two cases (40:9; 52:7) appears as something to be preached as part of the prophetic announcement of consolation. The question of the relationship between the messianic vindication theology of the interpreter and Jesus' understanding of the kingdom must be put off momentarily until other evidence is adduced, but a comparison of the latter three characteristics of Targumic kingdom usage with Jesus' usage is immediately possible.

For Jesus also the kingdom was essentially associated with God himself. This becomes inescapably clear when we consider such parables as those of the king settling his accounts (Matthew 18:23-35), the king who stages a wedding feast (Matthew 22:1-14) and the man, the seed and the earth (Mark 4:26-29). In each case Jesus portrays the kingdom in vividly realistic and personal terms as God's act of personal self-disclosure. In the first case, the king has mercy on one of his servants and overlooks a considerable debt, but the servant behaves meanly with one of his colleagues. Justly angry, the king punishes the servant because he has failed to act as mercifully as his lord. In the second instance, the king mounts a wedding feast, but the invited guests fail to attend. He therefore calls other guests: the joy of this occasion must be realized. But those who come must be properly attired (cf. 22:11-14). In the third parable, the imagery of a farmer, soil and seed expresses the mysterious and inevitable revelation of the kingdom; it joins the other two parables (and many others, of course) in setting out what it means for God to be king. In all three, the kingdom is not portrayed as a static entity; rather, something happens in the story, and just this happening conveys what God as king is like. Through the event of the parable we are told something about God which was not implicit from the beginning, and in this sense we can say they concern the disclosure of what it means for God to be king.

In the first two parables of God's kingship cited, the king acts on behalf of his good name: the unforgiving servant and the unworthy guests are punished. Forgiveness and festivity are freely offered, but there is considerable discipline involved in accepting them. To be forgiven in the conception of the first parable implies that one acknowledges one's own guilt, and appeals to the mercy of the offended party. A forgiven person lives on mercy, and mercy alone; he has foregone any appeal to his rights, because by a reckoning based on ordinary justice he deserves to be punished. If, then, such a person fails to act mercifully towards others, he has shown that he holds the king's mercy as something cheap. By invoking his right, he condemns himself; in Pauline language, he has reverted from grace to law. To be forgiven implies recognizing the rule of mercy and acting accordingly. There is no such thing as merely being forgiven: to accept forgiveness is to acknowledge as pre-eminent a new principle of living, and to leave a reckoning of what one is owed behind.

Similarly, there is more to attending a wedding feast than just being invited. The agreement to attend, and a willingness to prepare oneself (if this element is part of the original parable, cf. Jeremias [1972] p. 64) are also involved; the king's generosity must invoke a similar response in those who are invited if they are to enjoy the offer. Both these parables, using the image of an apparently arbitrary king, express the compelling logic of God's rule: his mercy and generosity need to be met in kind if they are to be accepted. God is depicted as actively intervening, as extending an offer which is more than a gift which can be received by a passive subject. The king acts in a new way, and his will is to be enacted as well as enjoyed just because he is the king, not just a benevolent patron. Difficult though it is to express, there is a compelling logic in Jesus' parables which conveys the need of repentance for anyone who wishes to take part in God's gracious offer.

The third parable mentioned is more complex, in that three images of the kingdom are introduced. It is commonly designated as the parable of the seed growing by itself, but this title is misleading. The seed quite evidently does not grow by itself: it is planted by a man in fruitful earth and grows by a process he does not really understand (4:26, 27). Steadily, however, the harvest comes, and when it arrives, he is ready to act (vv. 28, 29). The kingdom here is not something set up by the man; he sleeps as it unfolds. Yet his activity is involved in the total process, as is the fertility of the soil and the nature of the seed. The kingdom is related in the parable to the process of growth as a whole, and is identified with no single element in that process. Indeed, although the kingdom is at first compared to the man, whose steady labour is a reflection of God's patient toil in his creation, his reappearance at the end of the parable to reap the harvest is more reminiscent of the active participation by men in the kingdom, a theme which we have already observed in Jesus' parabolic teaching.

An analysis of the kingdom imagery in the parables could obviously be pressed much further (cf. Perrin [1976] and Weder [1978]); the examples cited here are only intended to illustrate the character of Jesus' kingdom teaching. The aspect of divine self-disclosure is clearly an element held in common with the Isaiah Targum, but in Jesus' preaching it is much more emphatically a personal self-disclosure, and is portrayed much more concretely than is the case in the Targum. The kingdom in Jesus' parables is consistently depicted either within real (Mark 4:26-29) or easily imaginable (Matthew 18:23-35; 22:1-14) circumstances. (Even the apparently whimsical actions of the kings would not contradict the expectation Jesus' first hearers probably had of how their rulers might behave [cf. Mark 6:17-29].) Jesus speaks of how the kingdom actually is in present experience, not only of how it will be in the future (cf. Targum Isaiah 24:23; 31:4). Even though the Targumic interpreter could conceive of the kingdom as something the prophets would one day preach as a present reality (cf. 40:9; 52:7), for him it was at the moment a matter of expectation, while for Jesus it was essentially a matter of experience (although not merely of present experience).

The revelation of the kingdom, then, is also for Jesus a present reality, and he accordingly preaches it himself (Mark 1:15; Matthew 4:17, 23; 9:35; Luke 4:43; 8:1) and sends others out to do so (Matthew 10:7; Luke 9:2, 6; 10:9, 11). What is for the Targumic interpreter a programme for the future implicit in the scripture becomes for Jesus an explicit activity designed to manifest the kingdom of God. He even understood his own ministry of healing to be a reflection of God's self-disclosure (cf. Matthew 12:28; Luke 11:20). In respect of the three characteristics of Targumic kingdom theology mentioned above, therefore, we can detect a certain intensification in the teaching of Jesus as given in the Gospels. God's personal intervention is depicted more realistically and vividly; his self-revelation is held to be immediate, and not only for the future; his rule is accordingly now to be preached, and not only predicted. Naturally, Jesus cannot be said to have removed the future element from the understanding of the kingdom current in his day; we have already called attention to Matthew 8:11, 12, where the future aspect of the kingdom is unmistakably emphasized, and modern critics have repeatedly and rightly insisted that such an emphasis was characteristic of Jesus. For Jesus, however, an assertion in respect of the future of the kingdom was an assertion made on the basis of its existential reality, and not only — as in the Targum — a matter of putting one's hope in a certain understanding of the scripture. In the end, the kingdom teaching of the Targum is exegetically based, while that of Jesus is experientially based. The implications of this distinction are to be explored in part three (Jesus' Style of Preaching Scripture as Fulfilled).

The theology of messianic vindication which the Targum expresses was occasioned by the hard events around 70 A.D., a generation after Jesus' death, so it is only to be expected that he did not echo this aspect of the Targumic kingdom theology. Indeed, he challenged the scribal notion that the messiah was to be a triumphal figure in the manner of David. In a well-known episode, he claimed that scripture itself confutes the equation between the messiah and the "son of David" (Matthew 22:41-45; Mark 12:35-37; Luke 20:41-44; cf. Chilton [1982²]). This, of course, raises questions as to what Jesus meant by "messiah" and "son of David," and how his understanding relates to the later Christian claim that he was both of these. Precisely because the passage does not accord entirely with later Christian preaching, however, its authenticity as a saying of Jesus seems reasonably assured, and the contradiction of the scribal teaching about the messiah, evidenced also in the seventeenth chapter of the *Psalms of Solomon*, is manifest.

Moreover, Jesus is portrayed in the Gospels as offering fellowship to groups of people that some of his contemporaries thought should be excluded. A good general example of such controversy is the dispute over Jesus' agreement to eat with tax-collectors (who were implicated in the unholy Roman occupation of Israel) and other "sinners" (Matthew 9:10-13; Mark 2:15-17; Luke 5:29-32). The comparatively open attitude of Jesus led even Gentiles to believe that they were not excluded from his ministry. One of the most surprising stories in the Gospel tradition is that of a Gentile woman who asks Jesus to heal her daughter (Matthew 15:21-28; Mark 7:24-30). Jesus at first refuses on the grounds that what is intended for the children (that is, of Israel) should not be given to dogs. But the woman is quick-witted as well as insistent, and replies that even dogs enjoy at least the crumbs under the table! Jesus' own reaction to this rejoinder is not noted, except to say that he praised her and complied with her original request.

This is the only instance in the New Testament in which Jesus is bested in argument, and the crucial question at issue is that of the scope of his ministry. Luke, who is keener than Matthew or Mark to stress the omniscience of Jesus, does not provide us with a version of this story. (The fact that John also does not hand on the story is not as remarkable. John seems to have followed traditions about Jesus which were largely independent of the traditions used in the first three Gospels. Matthew, Mark and Luke, on the other hand, are so similar to one another that they can relatively simply be printed in parallel columns so that the contents of one Gospel can be compared directly with those of the other two. Such a book is called a Synopsis of the Gospels, while the Gospels themselves are called "Synoptic." The phrase "the Synoptic Problem" refers to the fact that, while the first three Gospels are comparable, they are distinctive in their wording, the material they contain, and their order of presentation, cf. Styler [1982].) Luke's omission is perhaps less surprising than Matthew's and Mark's willingness to hand on this account of the successful contradiction of Jesus by a Gentile woman. In the following chapters in both Gospels (Matthew 16:13-20; Mark 8:27-30; and cf. Luke 9:18-22) we read of Jesus' question to his disciples about his own identity. The instance is unique, and the emphasis of Jesus on his identification with "the son of man" is quite distinct from the preferred usage ("christ," or "messiah") of a later period. In Matthew and Mark, this account of an inquiry into Jesus' identity in respect of God is placed in Caesarea Philippi, that is, in unequivocally Gentile territory, bearing the title of the Roman Emperor. In all of these important examples of Jesus' attitude towards those on the fringes of or outside Judaism, the New Testament traditions ascribe to him an orientation which is quite unlike the fiercer nationalism of the Isaiah Targum.

Our finding in regard to Jesus' understanding of the scope of God's action as compared to the Targumic theology of messianic vindication does not, however, permit of any easy generalizations to the effect that Jesus, in his universalism, was unlike the Judaism of his time. As we have seen, the Targumic theology is occasioned by political, social and religious circumstances which Jesus himself did not have to endure, so that a comparison along these lines would be anachronistic. Moreover, there are two further considerations in the light of which such a conclusion appears misleading.

In the first place, the story about the Gentile woman in Matthew and Mark is difficult to reconcile with the supposition that Jesus held to the same attitude towards Gentiles all through his ministry. The drama of the passage is generated by the alteration in Jesus' attitude, an alteration which Matthew's version magnifies, in that Jesus at first tells the woman, "I am sent only to the lost sheep of the house of Israel" (15:24). (Using similar words, Jesus in Matthew 10:6 limits the ministry of the twelve apostles to "the lost sheep of the house of Israel." At the end of the Gospel [28:19], the resurrected Jesus tells the eleven, "make disciples of all nations," so that a definite development in the understanding of the proper scope of the ministry initiated by Jesus is also presupposed in respect of mission. Cf. Walker [1967].) It is therefore inappropriate to ascribe an easy or consistent universalism to Jesus.

In the second place, Targumic interpretations which are demonstrably older than the Isaiah Targum offer a less circumscribed view of the kingdom. At Zechariah 14:9 and at Obadiah 21, the Prophetic Targums read:

> the kingdom of the LORD will be revealed upon all the dwellers of the earth.

As an interpretation, in the first instance, of Zechariah 14:9 this reading is quite understandable, since the Hebrew text declares, "the LORD will be king upon all the earth." The addition of the explicit reference to those who dwell on the earth, however, leaves the Targumic rendering more open to a universalistic understanding than the Hebrew text is. The Hebrew text of Obadiah 21 does not even refer to the earth, so that the use of the clause by the interpreter is even more striking here, and suggests that it was something of a conventional statement used in connection with the kingdom at the time this Targum was being produced. The association between the kingdom and Zechariah 14:9 is attested as early as the first century in a dictum of a rabbi named Eliezer ben Hyrcanos (in the ancient midrash to Exodus called the Mekhilta [17:14]), so that the possibility cannot be excluded that this rather more universalistic view of the kingdom, which is even more similar to Jesus' than that voiced in the Isaiah Targum, is characteristic of first century Judaism.

(All of the kingdom passages in the Prophetic Targums are treated in Chilton [1978] and [1982]). In other words, the differences between Jesus and the Isaiah Targum may just be a function of their different historical contexts: it would be uncritical to leap to making global theological claims about the relation between Jesus and Judaism on the basis of such differences.

At the same time, these differences underline the difficulty of comparing Jesus' teaching with the Isaiah Targum. On the one hand, the Targum seems—in its preservation of renderings which present the kingdom in terms of God himself, acting on behalf of his people—to contain traditions which shed light on the kingdom concept used by Jesus. Yet on the other hand, the Targum—in its clear expression of the nationalism of the period c. 70 A.D. and later — has a perspective which is shaped by events unknown to Jesus. Direct comparison between the theology of Jesus and that of the Targum would be anachronistic at best, and could easily distort our understanding of either. We might imagine Jesus was reacting to an idea which was only developed later, or falsely suppose that the Targum reflects precisely the sort of Judaism that is mentioned in the New Testament. For this reason, the attempt to investigate the relationship between Jesus and the Targum should, in the first instance, consider only those New Testament passages in which Jesus appears to cite Targumic traditions verbatim.

The procedure used for identifying such instances for the purpose of this book was straightforward. Initially, all cases in the Gospels in which Jesus cites or alludes to the book of Isaiah were noted. Editions of the New Testament in Greek have, for hundreds of years, presented marginal annotations of Old Testament passages which might have influenced the wording of verses in the New Testament. Frequently, these references are gathered together at the end of the edition, with the Old Testament passages cited sequentially along with the New Testament passages which cite or allude to them. A consideration of these notes, as presented for example in the twenty-sixth edition of the

Nestel-Aland Greek New Testament (1979), is in itself rewarding, because it reminds us of the extent to which the New Testament presupposes a knowledge of the Old Testament: it was not, on the whole, written to serve as a complete handbook of the faith for the uninitiated, but to ensure that those who confessed the faith held fast to its basic principles. Among these were the traditions about Jesus gathered together in the New Testament, and the insistence that the belief of Israel—expressed in the Old Testament and rightly admired throughout the ancient world—found its fulfilment in Jesus. Even a quick perusal of the number of explicit citations of the Old Testament in the New establishes this point beyond a doubt, and testifies to the impossibility of understanding the New Testament without reference to the faith and the documents of Israel.

Not all of the references noted in the latest Nestle-Aland edition, however, constitute citations of the Old Testament. (Indeed, the index heading refers to "Loci citati vel allegati," p. 739.) "Allusions" are also noted, and it is enormously difficult to set down precise criteria of what constitutes an allusion. Sometimes one finds only a word or two shared in an Old and a New Testament passage, but the term or terms in question are so distinctive that an allusion is posited. Sometimes very common words, not peculiar to or even characteristic of the Old Testament passage cited in Nestle-Aland appear in a New Testament passage, but the context of the usage is said to constitute it as an allusion. There are even cases in which the mere use of generally biblical imagery is claimed to allude to a specific biblical passage. The Nestle-Aland edition at least attempts to make the distinction between quotations (noted in italics) and allusions (set in normal type), but as is observed in its "Introduction" (p. 72), the distinction between a quotation and an allusion is frequently a matter of debate.

The reliance on learning from memory in the ancient world, and the relatively limited amount of material one was expected to learn (as compared to the deluge of written information confronting every literate person since the invention of movable type) guarantees that an educated

Church-goer at the end of the first century would notice more Old Testament quotations and allusions in the New Testament than an educated Church-goer in our century. But it is not at all clear that even a rabbi from the ancient period could draw up the lists of quotations and allusions available today, and tabulated with the aid of concordances and other (sometimes electronic) secondary resources. Even educated people in the first century would not normally be able to afford the library a theological student is expected to have today, so that the exact comparison of texts could also not be carried out easily. A degree of restraint, then, should be exercised in deciding whether a quotation of or allusion to the Old Testament is present in the New Testament. We must ask: (1) would an educated reader in the ancient period, familiar with the Old Testament but without benefit of specialized tools for study, understand the reference as a quotation or allusion? Then we need to pursue the matter further: (2) where a quotation or allusion is present, what difference does that make to an understanding of the passage? Unless we can clearly say (1) why we think the Old Testament is cited or alluded to in a given passage and (2) how the identification of the citation or allusion clarifies the meaning of the passage, there seems little point in calling attention to the phenomenon.

In preparation for the present study, every quotation of and allusion to Isaiah in sayings of Jesus given in the Nestle-Aland edition and in the edition of the United Bible Societies (1968) was subjected to the two strictures cited above. The next step was to determine whether the text of Jesus' saying had any demonstrable affinity with the Isaiah Targum. Obviously, some degree of affinity was inevitable, since in both the Targum and (according to the indices checked) the saying of Jesus, the book of Isaiah is at issue, but are there elements in Jesus' saying which are peculiarly Targumic? In order to answer that question, other ancient versions of the Old Testament also had to be consulted, and compared with the dominical saying and the Targum: the Hebrew (Masoretic) text, the Greek (Septuagint) text, the Latin (Vulgate) text and the Syriac (Peshitta) text. By following this procedure, one avoids the danger of attributing general similarity between the dominical saying and the Isaian text to the specific famliarity of Jesus with the Targumic tradition.

By means of this method, we shall posit the dependence of certain sayings of Jesus on the interpretation of Isaiah available today in the Targum. The argument is not that Jesus, the early preachers of his message, or the Evangelists actually used the Targum; if our analysis of its chronology is correct, this is out of the question. The evidence permits only of the conclusion that some interpretative traditions, later incorporated in the Targum, had a formative influence on the wording of some of the sayings of Jesus. The evidence here adduced is presented under two main headings:

A Instances of dictional coherence with the Targum
   1 in dominical references to Isaiah;
B Instances of thematic coherence with the Targum
   1 in dominical references to Isaiah.

By "dictional coherence" we mean a substantive verbal similarity, not only in respect of a few words, and naturally we are only concerned with cases in which Jesus' sayings contain dictional elements which are peculiar to the Targum. Instances of coherence of the type designated "A1" were discovered by the method described above: express dominical citations of Isaiah were compared with the Targum and other versions of the Old Testament, and instances of important agreement with the Targum isolated. By "thematic coherence" (treated under sayings of the "B1" type) we mean that the idea expressed by means of the dominical citation of Isaiah better corresponds to the wording of the Targum than to that of other ancient versions. Clearly, coherence of the "A1" type is more compelling evidence of a connection between the Targum and the dominical sayings than coherence of the "B1" type, since the judgment of thematic similarity is rather more subjective than the observation of verbal agreement. Nonetheless, the number of cases under "A1" leads to the conclusion that Targumic

traditions have contributed to the dictional shape of dominical sayings, and it would be arbitrary in the face of such
evidence not to inquire whether these traditions have also
contributed some of the themes expressed in the sayings.
Both of the main headings will later be subdivided (hence
the use of "1" with "A" and "B"), but initially the evidence so
far categorized should be cited in detail.

A final preliminary point, however, must be considered
before we can speak of Jesus' use of traditions contained in
the Isaiah Targum. The problem of determining when a
saying attributed to Jesus in the New Testament reflects
Targumic interpretation is relatively straightforward when
compared to the question: did Jesus actually say what the
New Testament claims he did? The question of the historicity of the New Testament, which reaches its most acute
form in the doubt that Jesus even existed, has been treated
repeatedly in the course of modern critical discussion. Any
competently written history of first century Christianity (for
example, Bruce [1969] pp. 163-167) will demonstrate that
not only Jesus' followers, but also ancient Jewish (Josephus,
and the authors of the so-called "Generations of Jesus") and
pagan (Tacitus, Suetonius) writers accepted as a matter of
course that Jesus existed. Those who refused to accept his
message did so openly, without recourse to the modern
expedient of pretending he never lived.

Of course, the mere fact that Jesus existed is no guarantee
that every passage in the New Testament is, by modern
standards, historical. "History," the understanding of past
human events within a framework of cause and effect, is for
us a science to some extent. We demand evidence before we
accept that a given event actually occurred, and we also ask
that the event be explained in a way that makes it plausible
to us. Certain of the events connected with Jesus, for example his preaching of the kingdom, his calling of disciples, his
development of a wide following, his controversies with
religious authorities, the open conflict between Jesus and
those authorities and his consequent crucifixion, are easily
accepted as historical, although the task of defining these
events precisely and assessing their significance remains. On

the other hand, the descriptions in the New Testament of Jesus' birth or his exorcisms, and accounts such as the feeding of the five thousand, the transfiguration and above all the resurrection, confront us with claims about Jesus which do not have analogies in our ordinary experience. Should we, therefore, dismiss the Gospels entirely as historical sources? If we do so, we are left with the quandary of what to do with the Gospel material which seems clearly to be historical. Moreover, in order to be consistent, we would have also to dismiss Tacitus and Josephus as historical sources, because they report such odd happenings as exorcisms (cf. *The History* 4:81; *Antiquities* 8:46). The difficulty of dealing with apparently historical documents which record events outside our usual experience is not, that is to say, peculiar to the evaluation of the New Testament, or even of the Bible as a whole.

In reading any ancient source, one is brought face to face with an understanding of reality in some respects different from his own. Narratives of exorcisms provide a good example of this, because they are widely reported in the ancient world, and yet strike most readers today as decidedly odd. There are two short cuts through the dilemma which remain widely current. By the nineteenth century, a confident consensus ruled in intellectual circles, according to which the universe could be explained on the basis of physical cause and effect, without recourse to the postulation of external or supernatural forces. New Testament scholars in this period largely followed the example of those earlier Enlightenment critics who devalued or denied the importance of the miraculous in the sources they studied. Those who continue to accept this rationalist or positivist approach will simply refuse to accept accounts of exorcisms when they appear in the Gospels on the grounds that such events do not happen in our world. To others, however, it seems arrogant to suppose that we are in any position to claim that modern views of reality are exhaustive, and that therefore accounts which do not accord with them are false. Rather than take our relativistic scientific findings as a standard, it is frequently claimed, we should accept biblical accounts as the historical records they claim to be. Depending on the short cut one takes, one will come to very different positions on exorcism (and much else) in the New Testament. Although the two short cuts, or variants on them, can be instanced in many treatments of the Gospels, both are in the end unsatisfactory. The first is in fact not a historical method at all, but is simply the outcome of measuring the Gospel traditions according to a pseudo-scientific standard. To say that exorcism is illusory, and that therefore ancient documents do not reliably describe any, is to use a second-hand, unverified notion of what can and cannot occur instead of analyzing what the text to hand actually wishes to say. But the method of many conservative evangelicals also tends to sacrifice the text to an a priori proposition. To claim without qualification that biblical documents attempt to provide historical records and must be treated as such is an assertion which is strange for two reasons. First, even if it is the attempt of biblical documents to report reliably in our modern critical sense, we have no guarantee that they are successful in that attempt. (By the same argument, we would have to accept as historical the scores of exorcism narratives in Jewish, Graeco-Roman, Patristic and Medieval literature.) Second, the assertion places the Bible under an immense constraint in that its authority or inspiration is held to reside only in its historicity, so that it is not permitted to be anything but historical. The rationalist position insists that biblical exorcism narratives cannot be something the conservative position declares they must be.

What is most disturbing about this impasse is that exegesis, the art of reading texts so that their own concerns are understood, is avoided by both positions. Rather than lay down what the Bible may or may not say, we need to attend to the texts themselves in order to discern the nature of what they say and their message. The nature of a text is as important as its message, indeed the message cannot be determined unless one appreciates how it is conveyed. To take the example of the story about the Gentile woman and Jesus (Matthew 15:21-28; Mark 7:24-30), which has already been mentioned, we have the advantage of having two versions of the passage, which helps us better to see both its nature and its message. The variants between the two versions make it quite apparent that each has a distinctive theological meaning within its respective Gospel. To make but one comparison, for Matthew (15:22) the woman is a Canaanite, while for Mark (7:26) she is a Greek from Syro-Phoenicia. This difference corresponds to the particular interests of the two Evangelists. "Canaanite" is a description using a category from the Old Testament for someone who resides in Israel, but does not belong to the covenant community, and Matthew is precisely concerned with the membership of Israel (15:24, cf. 10:6). To say, on the other hand, that the woman is a Greek from outside Israel points ahead to Jesus' significance for Gentiles, and in fact Mark is written from a non-Jewish perspective (cf. 7:3).

One or both Evangelists did not necessarily alter the story; since we have no direct access to the traditional material handed down to them, perhaps by word of mouth, it is impossible to be certain as to the extent to which they may have preserved versions of the story which were already distinctive before they wrote. Luke, the only Evangelist to speak of his sources, refers to "eyewitnesses and ministers of the word" (1:2), not to written documents, so that a certain degree of variety in the Jesus tradition prior to the Evangelists is to be supposed. Nothing is related directly about the Evangelists in the New Testament; unfortunately, we must wait until the second century for such information, and then the sources in question seem largely to be dependent on legend. For this reason, we can only get back to the methods and concerns of the Evangelists by inference, observing differences between their Gospels and the characteristics of each. It is therefore common to speak of "Mark" in comparison to "Matthew," for example, as a way of contrasting the distinctive material and presentation of one Gospel as compared to another. This need not imply that the individual Evangelists are responsible for all of the differences among the Synoptic Gospels, or the Gospels generally. Whether or not we explain the difference between Mark and Matthew in the manner of referring to the woman as a matter of redactional alteration, the point seems inescapable that what at first may appear to be a purely historical detail (when viewed in isolation within each Gospel) proves on minimal analysis to bear a theological meaning. The story illustrates the attitude of Jesus towards Gentiles, but what sort of Gentiles? The two Gospels give Jesus' attitude a distinctive colouring according to the details with which the story is presented and the context within which it appears. In a word, the story is an example of a Jewish story genre we have already encountered: haggadah.

The category of haggadah does not in any sense exclude the possibility that historical information may be present, but it does imply that in the first instance such a story must be evaluated according to the principle it illustrates, and not on the supposition that it is a deliberately historical record. The story reflects the character of its principal, much as the story of Johanan ben Zakkai leaving Jerusalem, greeting Vespasian and going to Yavneh (see above, on Giṭṭin 56a, b). The attitude of Jesus in the story, particularly because it is changed because of what the Gentile woman says, represents a different stance from the Church's, in which—as we have already remarked—Gentile mission was taken as a matter of course as part of the basic Christian programme. This is noteworthy from a historical point of view. Marc Bloch, the distinguished French historian, compared a good historian to a lawyer. He cross-examines his witness, and is particularly alert to the possibility that an unusual detail, which might cast new light on the proceedings, might crop up quite unexpectedly in the testimony. The witness might in all good faith think his testimony has one meaning (e.g., that a defendant is guilty), and yet say something which bears quite another meaning (e.g., that he is innocent). "Guilt" and "innocence" are obviously not historical categories, in that history concerns what happened, not what should or should not have happened, but the analogy between historical sources and legal testimony is useful (cf. Bloch [1976] pp. 60-69). In the present case, our "witnesses" have, as it were, let slip something about the stance of Jesus which we would not have known otherwise: that he developed his attitude to Gentiles under pressure. The reaction to his preaching was such as to drive him beyond limits he himself would ordinarily have respected. This "cross-examination" of sources is sometimes (cf. Tuckett [1980] p. 36), but mistakenly, called "the criterion of dissimilarity" in New Testament research. In fact, this criterion was described and developed by Norman Perrin as a tool for analyzing sayings of Jesus, not for making direct historical judgments about him (Perrin [1967] p. 39). Sayings analysis will concern us below; the concern at the moment is simply to point out that the example haggadah stands out under ordinary historical consideration as a good witness to the attitude of Jesus. The circumstance in which this attitude is said to have been expressed is that of an exorcism. Matthew (15:22) and Mark (7:25, 26) agree that the demonic possession of her daughter caused the woman to seek Jesus' help in the first place. In the ancient period, demons were thought of as causative agents of disease (somewhat as we, most of us without evidence, imagine that bacteria and viruses are the cause of many of our complaints), and in fact Matthew describes the daughter as healed (15:28) rather than saying that the demon was cast out (cf. Mark 7:29, 30). Nonetheless, the attitude of Jesus —which seems historical — is given an undeniably exorcistic setting.

Is the exorcism also to be considered historical? As the very means by which an attitude of Jesus which seems historical found expression, we must at least say that this exorcism story is historically significant: for us it marks a watershed in the development of the Jesus movement from a phenomenon within early Judaism to an international religion. Moreover, because the exorcism is presented as the very occasion on which Jesus expressed this attitude, it appears to be historically meaningful: that is, the exorcism was taken by Jesus' followers to imply a new attitude to Gentiles, and their acceptance of the attitude influenced the subsequent course of events. As used here, historical "significance" is a category that refers to the value we attach to a human event. Whatever we think of Jesus or Christianity, the significance of this story (the "human event" in question) for the development of religion in the West is obvious. Historical "meaning" is a somewhat different matter, referring to the value attached to the event by those who were closest to it in time. Jesus' followers attached immense value to this exorcism, and acted on its implications. If — as seems likely, given Jesus' surprising change of attitude in the story — the story does go back to eyewitnesses, then they saw what they called an exorcism take place, and their subsequent action (including telling the story) makes the exorcism historically meaningful. But the adjective "historical" is commonly used in a third sense, to describe what actually occurred (as distinct from the fantastic, mythical or imaginary). Did Jesus successfully exorcise a demon in the vicinity of Tyre (Matthew 15:21; Mark 7:24)?

At this point the historian, just because he is a historian, must be circumspect. He cannot prove that demons do or do not exist, since that is a natural scientific judgment, and to ask him to do so after nearly two thousand years is out of the question. He can, however, point out that the story is not fantastic; the characters and events are not portrayed as beyond the expectations of normal (if not ordinary) experience as reflected in ancient literature. Further, the story is no myth; the conventions of the gods or a god entering human experience in order to influence the natural world are absent. Lastly, the principals and the setting are quite concrete, and not in the least imaginary. By contrast, the haggadah of Moses in his conference with God (see Menahoth 29b) begins and ends on an imaginary note, and therefore should not be considered historical in the third sense discussed. But the historian is, quite simply, pressed by the nature of the evidence to hand to say that this historically significant and meaningful exorcism story was occasioned by something that happened which Jesus' contemporaries saw as an exorcism. They saw a palpable evil overcome by Jesus, and they experienced this as an exorcism. (What we would have experienced it as, given our no doubt more useful understanding of the world, cannot be said with anything like certainty.) The human event (the text and its effect on subsequent events) presupposes and reflects an actual occurrence. To claim more would go beyond the brief of historical thinking, while an insistence on claiming less would perhaps betray a dogmatic rationalism.

Our discussion of the historical value of the New Testament traditions about Jesus would naturally have to be pressed much further, and detailed investigation undertaken, in order to deal competently with the range and complication of the stories told about him. The remarks offered above are intended only to introduce the question, and also to point out the relatively straightforward nature of analyzing the sayings of Jesus as compared to evaluating stories told about him. That Jesus taught, and that his words were precious to his disciples, is obvious, and we do not have the same conceptual difficulty in dealing with assertions of the type, "Jesus said such and so," as we do with assertions of the type, "Jesus exorcised such and such a demon."

The student of Jesus' words must nonetheless reckon with the fact that the Evangelists and their predecessors were not interested simply in the verbatim transcription of what Jesus said. For them, his words were filled with meaning, and they handed them on so as to highlight that meaning. They selected which to present from the traditions known to them, provided the sayings selected with contexts, and used the wording which seemed to them best suited to convey the meaning intended. Two crucial examples from the Synoptic Gospels may suffice to illustrate this point: what were the first and last public words of Jesus?

According to Matthew (4:17) and Mark (1:15), Jesus' initial announcement after his baptism concerned the kingdom of God (or, as Matthew has it, "of the heavens" — a Jewish periphrasis for God, used to avoid any danger that the divine name might openly be pronounced). But in Matthew, Jesus' announcement — identical to that of John the Baptist (3:2) — opens with a reference to repentance, and Matthew presents the announcement as a whole in the context of the statement that Jesus' activity corresponded to a promise of salvation in the book of Isaiah (4:12-16). The three peculiar features of Matthew's presentation of Jesus' initial kingdom preaching correspond to his tendency to present John and Jesus as witnesses to the same message (cf. 3:7 and 12:34; 23:33; 3:10 and 7:19; 3:12 and 13:30), to his emphasis on the ethical component of Jesus' teaching, and to his liking for citations from the Old Testament which are said to be "fulfilled" in Jesus' ministry.

Mark, on the other hand, presents a mention of repentance only after the kingdom reference in Jesus' first preaching, and does not refer to any announcement of the kingdom by John, or to Jesus' fulfilment of a specific scripture. In Mark, Jesus comes to Galilee after John's arrest (1:14), and announces that the time is fulfilled, as well as the coming of the kingdom (v. 15). Moreover, he calls men to repent *and* to believe in this gospel. The emphasis here is on the fresh start represented by Jesus' ministry, a start which leads immediately to the calling of disciples to help in the mission (vv. 16-20).

Luke's presentation of Jesus' initial preaching diverges from both Matthew's and Mark's and is the most sophisticated of the three. Luke gives a rather full description of Jesus' activity in a synagogue in Nazareth as part of his itinerant ministry (4:16-30), and a christological orientation is apparent. Jesus cites a passage from Isaiah in the synagogue, and claims he has been anointed to fulfill the divine commission spoken of by the prophet (vv. 18-21). Astonishment about this claim — together with his insistence that Gentiles are favoured by God — then leads the congregation to the abortive attempt to execute Jesus (vv. 22-30). It is noteworthy that the public ministry of Paul in Acts (which was also written by Luke, cf. 1:1-2 and the opening of the Gospel) closes with a citation from Isaiah and a reference to the inclusion of Gentiles in God's salvation (28:25-28). The two motives of scriptural fulfilment and mission to the Gentiles are obviously interwoven, and the identity of Jesus stands at the centre of both. Luke's sophistication, however, does not only reside in his skilful orchestration of related ideas; he also alludes to Jesus' kingdom preaching without actually citing it. In Luke 4:43, he has Jesus say "I must also tell the good news of God's kingdom in other cities, because I have been sent for this purpose." The kingdom is assumed to be the basic concept of his ministry even though Jesus has not so far expressly referred to it in the Gospel. In Acts 28:31, Paul is also said to preach the kingdom, and indeed in 20:25 a saying attributed to Paul presents the kingdom as a characteristic component of his ministry in a way reminiscent of the Jesus saying in Luke 4:43. Save for a brief mention of the kingdom by Paul in Acts 14:22, however, one would not have guessed from Luke's overall portrayal of his ministry (apart from 20:25 and 28:31, that is) that the kingdom was so important to Paul. Clearly, Luke presupposes that his readers have some familiarity with the message of Jesus and of Paul, and feels able to allude to more than he expressly relates from the tradition before him. In so doing, he joins the other two Synoptic Evangelists in shaping the introduction of Jesus' public ministry in a way that reflects and expresses their own theological concerns.

"My God, my God, why have you forsaken me?" As reported by Matthew (27:46) and Mark (15:34), these are the last words of Jesus from the cross. In both Gospels, Jesus' contemporaries misunderstand his call to "my God" in Aramaic as a call for help from the biblical prophet Elijah (Matthew 27:47; Mark 15:35); Elijah is said in the Old Testament itself not to have died, but to have been taken up alive into heaven (2 Kings 2:11), and in Jewish tradition it was believed he could aid the pious in times of need. Jesus then dies after crying aloud (Matthew 27:50; Mark 15:37). Both Matthew and Mark refer to a tear in the veil of the Temple (Mathew 27:51a; Mark 15:38); this serves as a vindication of Jesus' prophecy against the Temple (in Matthew 24, Mark 13 and Luke 21) which would have been especially significant to readers who knew that the tear in the curtain was only the beginning, that the Temple had in fact been destroyed. For Mark, the stark image of the dead Jesus and the torn curtain are the occasion for the confession of the centurion, "Truly, this man was God's son" (15:39). Jesus' true identity, precisely as he dies, becomes evident to the

Gentile, and indeed the manner of the death is said to prompt the exclamation. The officer knows and confesses the truth the reader has known from the beginning of the Gospel (1:1), that Jesus is God's son. But this disclosure has been gradually developed through the Gospel, and—significantly—only a Gentile (and a Roman, at that) voices the proper identification, and then only when Jesus has died.

Although Matthew has the officer say almost the same thing (27:54), the context in which he says it is quite different. After his mention of the torn curtain, Matthew alone among the Evangelists reports an earthquake, tombs opening, and a resurrection of "many bodies of the dead saints" (27:51b-53). Matthew's inclusion of this material at just this point seems to some degree artificial, because he admits that the "saints" only appeared in Jerusalem after Jesus' resurrection (27:53). Nonetheless, "the earthquake and the things that were happening" (or — even more confusingly — "had happened," as in many good Greek manuscripts of the New Testament) are given as the occasion for what the officer and those with him say. In Matthew, Jesus is publicly vindicated even at the moment of his death; Mark's image of the forsaken son is transformed into that of the son as judge (cf. Matthew 25:31-46, which is unique to this Gospel), at least in anticipation.

Contextually, then, Jesus' last words in Matthew and Mark bear rather different meanings. In Mark, they are part of the pattern within the entire crucifixion scene of references or allusions to Psalm 22 (and 69) in portraying the forsakenness of the son. But Psalm 22, after its opening complaint, turns to praise in view of God's help (cf. vv. 22-31): where is God's help to be seen in Mark's Gospel? The narrative closes with the silence of the women who discovered the empty tomb (16:8, vv. 9-20) being an obviously later addition to the Gospel), so that the reader is turned back to his own experience to await the promised vindication, and to the picture of sonship in suffering which Mark so vividly draws. Mark offers no simple answer to the question of Jesus' vindication; although the fact of his resurrection is confirmed, the reader is encouraged and challenged to discover the experience of resurrection beyond the written page in the path of Jesus (cf. 8:34). The case is different with Matthew. While he is no less express than Mark in his reliance on the Psalter to depict Jesus' crucifixion, he is comparatively unsubtle when it comes to describing Jesus' vindication. God, in effect, answers Jesus' cry in the earthquake and the multiple resurrections, and that on a scale so cosmic that it almost makes the appearance of the risen Jesus (Matthew 28:16-20, where the emphasis is on the teaching of the resurrected one, rather than on the fact of his resurrection) seem almost anticlimactic by comparison.

The differences between Matthew and Mark in respect of the portrayal of Jesus' death, although obviously significant, appear less striking when Luke's version is also considered. The dying Jesus here cries out in a great voice, and uses words from another psalm (31:6), "Father, into your hands I commend my spirit" (23:46). The mention of the Temple veil appears in the preceding verse, so that nothing stands between this statement and the centurion's confession (v. 47), which is also given in different words ("Truly, this man was just"; for the connection between being just and being God's son in Jewish tradition, cf. Wisdom 2:18). These alterations (as compared to Matthew and Mark) contribute to a focus on the nobility of the death of Jesus, as contrasted to Mark's stark portrait of his forsakenness and Matthew's early reference to his vindication.

The variations among the Synoptic Gospels in the way they open and close their accounts of Jesus' public ministry are important for any appreciation of the character and purpose of these documents. Obviously, our observations cannot be used to claim that Jesus did not preach the kingdom, or that he did not die with words from the book of Psalms on his lips. The agreement of the Evangelists in these respects is apparent, and — historically speaking — if Jesus did not preach the kingdom and die piously, the emergence of Christianity, with its many references and allusions to its founder's kingdom preaching and its insistence on preserving the inheritance of the Old Testament as Jesus did, even under pressure (cf. for example, Hebrews 5:7-10), is a phenomenon which is all but inexplicable. At the same time, Jesus can only have spoken one set of first words and one set of last words. In other cases, one might suggest that Jesus said more or less the same thing in distinctive ways on different occasions, and so explain deviations among the Synoptic Gospels (cf. J. M. Rist [1978]), although this solution can only appear rather fundamentalistic unless one also at least considers that such differences might be accounted for more easily as actual variations which emerged as the saying was transmitted in the early Church. In any case, that option cannot be used here, where the occasion of the words is given as the same in each Gospel, and any attempt to harmonize the accounts would be purely speculative: at most one of the Synoptic Evangelists accurately reports the first preaching of Jesus, and at most two have his last words right (and even then, the meaning of these words in Matthew and Mark, as determined by their contexts, is rather different). The differences between the Gospels in both cases cannot be written off as incidental, since — as we have seen — they correspond to important thematic streams in their respective presentations of Jesus, and together they make for more variety in the Gospel account of Jesus' first and last public utterances (without even bringing in for consideration the additional variations which John contains) than is consistent with the supposition that the Evangelists recorded the words of Jesus verbatim.

This brief consideration of the divergences among the Synoptic Gospels in respect of Jesus' first preaching and his last words from the cross scarcely yields a straightforward answer as to what he did actually say on those occasions. But it does demonstrate the necessity of a disciplined procedure when putting historical questions of this type to the New Testament. Matthew, Mark and Luke cannot all be accurate in these two cases, and because their portraits of the beginning and end of Jesus' ministry are consistent with their characteristic concerns throughout their Gospels, we have no ready-made way to hand of deciding that one of them is more "reliable" than the others, or that one is more governed by secondary literary factors than by a concern for "history." (By the use of quotation marks, we indicate how odd our notions would have seemed to the Evangelists; for them to be reliable clearly meant more than just telling what happened, and history was more concerned with significance and meaning than with actual occurrence.) The supposition that Mark was the literary source of Matthew and Luke has come under such severe fire that it is scarcely a solid foundation on which to build a historical conclusion (cf. Farmer [1964]), and even the long-held view that John was, as the last of the Gospels, dependent on the Synoptics, has been questionable at best for more than forty years (cf. P. Gardner-Smith [1938]).

To a significant extent, the inquiry into the literary relationships among the Gospels has been motivated by the desire to discover the earliest, historically most reliable Gospel, but the attempt has not succeeded. First of all, the assumption that there is a purely literary relationship among the Gospels is problematic. On this hypothesis, the Evangelists were highly literate authors with the materials and personnel available to mix and match sources, and yet (rather perversely) they do not consistently follow any one of those sources. Their behaviour was not only odd on this reconstruction, it also was not consistent with the early Jewish background of the New Testament, in which oral transmission, not professional literary activity, was the characteristic means of formal learning. (Appeals to the example of Josephus miss the point: he was a privileged quisling.) In this connection, it is noteworthy that there is a synoptic relationship among the Pentateuch Targums (cf. Chilton [1980[2]] and [1982[3]]); the possibility that it might be analogous to the better known New Testament Synoptic Problem has been suggested, but not yet tested fully. Secondly, even if one Gospel is prior to another from a literary point of view, it does not follow it is more historically reliable than its successors. The latter judgment depends on the intent of the writer and the information available to him; Luke, for example, quite evidently thought he could produce a more orderly account than his predecessors (cf. 1:1-4; whether or not he has Matthew and Mark in mind is another question), and as historians we can hardly assume that he failed just because he wrote after his predecessors.

Although the tendency to confuse literary judgments with historical judgments in New Testament study unfortunately remains, the simple facts cannot be ignored that (1) we cannot prove our Gospels stand in a relationship of purely literary dependence, nor do we know what exactly that (perhaps partly oral, partly literary) relationship consisted of and (2) we cannot use any of our hypothetical schemes of literary dependence as a pretext for ignoring some Gospel material and relying on other material in considering historical questions. What we can say with some certainty is that the Gospels — even in their records of Jesus' words — are not, in the modern sense, historical documents any more than they are, in the modern sense, fiction. In their haggadic representation of Jesus' words, reminiscence of the remembered tradition and anticipation of the ultimate significance of that tradition within the context of the particular portrait of faith developed in each Gospel are fused so as to illustrate what was distinctive or characteristic about Jesus. Indeed, the emphatic insistence at the end of each Gospel that Jesus' life and identity are on-going realities reveals that, for the Evangelists and their predecessors, the meaning of Jesus' words is at least as relevant for the present and the future as it was for the past. The purpose of the Gospels in respect of Jesus' words, then, is neither to note down exactly what was said nor to imagine what could have been said (in the manner of modern historians such as Gibbon or ancient historians such as Thucydides); they offer considered views of the meaning of Jesus' words for those who believe in him. How much in their presentations is the result of the interpretative activity of the Evangelists and their predecessors and how much reflects Jesus' message is to be decided by the critical examination of each passage; literary critical short cuts, such as the supposition that Mark's is the earliest Gospel and therefore must be the most historical, are simply no longer viable.

The considerations offered, by demonstrating the differences of emphasis and content among the Gospels, as well as by highlighting the importance and independent value of these different readings within each Gospel, clearly suggest that historical investigation must begin with the texts as we have them in all their variety, and not proceed from the supposition that they can be reduced to the content of a single source. As the historical value of a Gospel is determined, of course, and the findings collated with conclusions in respect of another Gospel, something like a consensus among the Gospels might be discovered, but that is a very different procedure from assuming from the beginning that we know the sources used by the Evangelists. Fundamentally, a historical method demands that we adopt a redaction critical procedure, at least to the extent that we acknowledge that we must work from our texts back to the tradition(s) used by the Evangelists, and from there to the historical Jesus. The question remains, how best can this be achieved?

In his book, *Rediscovering the Teaching of Jesus*, Norman Perrin championed the use of "the criterion of dissimilarity" in investigating the sayings of Jesus (cf. Perrin [1967], p. 39). As a follower of Perrin, one looks for those sayings which are dissimilar to the characteristic sentiments of Judaism and early Christianity. According to the logic of the criterion, since the Evangelists and their predecessors would have shaped Jesus' sayings to accord with the Judaism in which they were nurtured and the Christianity they came to espouse, sayings which do not reflect the concerns of these movements are those which are most likely to be authentic. The obvious difficulty with this criterion is that Jesus was a Jew, and his sayings were handed on most avidly by Christians (who were presumably influenced by his message), so that any such elimination of the Jewish and Christian elements in his teaching is bound to distort our impression of it disastrously. In fact, Perrin's portrayal of the essential message of Jesus consists largely and — given the inherent weakness of the "criterion of dissimilarity" —predictably of a repeated emphasis on what is said to be radically new (cf. pp. 107-108; 151-153; 203-206). But no new image of Jesus the historical figure is in this way posited by Perrin; on the contrary, an all too familiar Jesus is "rediscovered." He is reminiscent of the Jesus of the Gnostics, second century thinkers for whom the God of the Old Testament, the creator of the world, was essentially evil; in their view, the saviour god — associated with Jesus by Christian Gnostics — was quite different from this Jewish creator god. One Gnostic, named Marcion, actually produced his own truncated edition of the New Testament, which consisted of fragments of Paul's letters and parts of Luke's Gospel (the rest being excised as the result of secondary Jewish influence). No doubt inadvertently, Perrin is driving the same sort of wedge between the Old and New Testaments by applying his "criterion of dissimilarity," albeit in a more sophisticated way than Marcion ever intimated.

The great trouble with such "criteria" (cf. Stein [1980]) is that they promise much more than they can possibly deliver. "The criterion of dissimilarity" is a misleading, short cut attempt to identify the teaching of the historical Jesus (or the minimum of his teaching as Perrin has it, p. 20). The fact that a given saying, in its present context in a given Gospel, offers an account of faith which happens to be unlike what we should expect to find in an early Jewish or Christian source might very well be an indication of nothing other than our own ignorance about early Judaism and Christianity. And even if a saying is rather original and does not only appear so because we are imperfectly informed, we must ask: were not the Evangelists and their predecessors to some extent original? Although their creativity is on the whole that of interpreters rather than that of inventors, can we really assume (as a mechanical application of the "criterion of dissimilarity" would have us do) that Jesus was the only innovative theologian in the early Christian movement? In a word, this "criterion" helps us to discover what is unusual in the Gospel tradition, but not what is "historical" (that is, in Perrin's sense of the word, as referring to authentic words of Jesus); it does not even necessarily indicate that the material isolated is traditional rather than redactional, although in

most cases it is perhaps more likely the former. The use of
this criterion represents an attempt to reduce redaction
criticism and tradition criticism to the application of a
formula, but so much of the *evaluation* necessary to distinguish tradition from redaction and historical tradition from
interpretative tradition is absent that we cannot commend it
as a critical tool.

A critical approach to the question at hand demands that
we spurn such short cuts, and sift through our texts layer by
layer, assessing the part the Evangelist seems to have played
in shaping a given saying, the way the saying was viewed and
interpreted in the tradition before the Evangelist, and then
(and only then), how (or, whether) the saying was spoken by
Jesus, and what he meant by it. Even this characterization of
the stages of the critical process is schematic and simplified,
of course. At the redactional level, there might be more than
one work of edition behind the present form of a given
Gospel, while — at the traditional level —there is little
likelihood that only one interpretative school shaped a saying as handed on to its redactor(s). Finally, we cannot
exclude the possibilities that Jesus may have said more or
less the same thing on different occasions, so that different
forms of basically the same saying influenced one another,
or that he simply changed his mind from time to time, with
the result that earlier sayings were put in a new light or
altered by his disciples with regard to later sayings. In the
face of these uncertainties — which, given our understanding of the development of the New Testament, are very real,
and not in the least exaggerated here — one can scarcely
slice through the Gordian knot of tradition and redaction by
means of a "criterion" or two. Redaction criticism, tradition
criticism, and balanced historical judgment on the basis of
these two, are simply indispensable, no matter how much we
might prefer to use quicker methods.

The use of Targumic forms of citation from the Old
Testament in sayings ascribed to Jesus does permit us, however, at least in some cases to begin our investigation at the
level of tradition rather than at that of redaction. In general,
the Evangelists preferred to use versions of the Old Testa-

ment in Greek very much like the Septuagint, rather than Targums or Hebrew texts, in biblical citations (even in the context of Jesus' words). Although it is true that the correspondence between New Testament citations of the Old Testament and the Septuagint is not usually exact, we must remember that the text of the Septuagint was itself not completely fixed in the New Testament period. Further, when the variants of the Septuagint are also taken into account, the Evangelists agree much more with this Greek version in their Old Testament citations than with Aramaic or Hebrew versions. These simple facts are widely recognized in the cases of Mark (cf. Suhl [1965]), Luke (cf. Holtz [1968]) and John (cf. Freed [1965]), but as a result of the work of Krister Stendahl (1954) it is still commonly held that Matthew relied on the Hebrew text of the Old Testament. While it is true that some of the elements in Matthew's citation agree more with the Hebrew than with the Greek texts of the Old Testament available to us, many more of these elements agree with the Septuagint and its variants, so that it seems likely that Matthew relied on an emerging tradition of Old Testament translation very much like what ultimately crystalized as "the Septuagint" (cf. Johnson [1943], Rothfuchs [1969] and Chilton [1979] pp. 108-115).

The preference of the Evangelists for Septuagint-like versions of the Old Testament is hardly surprising. They were writing in Greek for Greek audiences, and used the Old Testament translation which their listeners or readers were most familiar with. Of course, at times the traditions they handed on were fixed in a different form in their Old Testament citations, and even reflected the Hebrew or Aramaic (rather than the Greek) wording fairly faithfully. The cases in which the Targum to Isaiah shines through the text of the Greek New Testament seem to be instances of just this situation, as we will see. Of course, it is always possible that the Evangelist may have known the Targum (if only indirectly) and used it from time to time; the fact that the Evangelists generally preferred Septuagintal forms of citation does not prove that they always did so. We shall see, however, that the citations of the Targum to Isaiah in the

New Testament record of Jesus' words make better sense as traditional elements in the dominical sayings than as redactional innovations.

The Targum is also of great importance because it helps us to type the sort of tradition we are dealing with: the early Jewish, Aramaic stratum of the New Testament stands immediately at the centre of attention. The step from stating that a saying has such a background to asserting it is an authentically dominical utterance is, in turn, a fairly short one. It is nonetheless a crucial step, and should only be taken consciously and critically; because the Aramaic tradents of Jesus' words were also interpreters of his message, we should be wary of any assumption (as, for example, seems to underlie parts of Jeremias' treatment of the parables [1972]) to the effect that "Aramaic" or "early Jewish" is synonymous with "dominical." The first two terms are used to express judgments as to the nature of tradition, the last is used to express a judgment of historical fact. Although — given the nature of the Gospels — the modern student will always have to rely on his judgment to distinguish Jesus' words from interpretative adaptations of those words, he can at least be clear in his own mind as to the sort of judgment he is called upon to make at each point in his investigation. Such clarity will help him to recognize where the points of uncertainty in his own analysis lie, and precisely in what ways and why he differs from other investigators. For these reasons, the reflection on our critical procedures offered above is a necessary preliminary to the analysis we now wish to undertake.

2. *Exegetical Studies*

A1 INSTANCES OF DICTIONAL COHERENCE WITH THE TARGUM IN DOMINICAL REFERENCES TO ISAIAH

In the Gospel according to Mark, Jesus gives an explanation of why he teaches in parables (4:11, 12). He tells those around him, more particularly the Twelve, "to you the mystery of the kingdom of God has been given, but to those outside all is in parables" (v. 11). To this explanation, a citation from the book of Isaiah is appended:

> so that seeing they might see and not perceive, and hearing they might hear and not understand, lest they reform and it be forgiven them (v. 12).

There are two outstanding problems connected with verse twelve. The first is that this "citation" is rather a loose rendering of the Isaian text, the second that Jesus appears to be saying that he tells parables in order that his message might *not* be understood. In both respects, the Targum to Isaiah can help us out of our difficulty.

In the Targum, Isaiah 6:9, 10 is rendered as follows:

> And he said, go and speak to this people that hear indeed but do not understand, and who see indeed but do not know. Make the heart of this people dull and their ears heavy and shut their eyes, lest they see with their eyes and hear with their ears and understand with their heart, and they repent, and it be forgiven them.

The clause, "and it be forgiven them," stands out, because it also appears in Mark 4:12, but not in other ancient versions of the Old Testament (which read "lest they reform [or "repent"] and I heal them"). Moreover, the reference in Mark 4:12 and Targum Isaiah 6:9 to the wilfully blind and deaf people of the Isaian text is as "they," while the other versions have them addressed directly as "you." Taken together, these observations seem amply to justify T. W. Manson's conclusion that the Markan citation of Isaiah depends on the Targum (Manson [1955] pp. 76-80; the partial similarity of the Peshitta at this point is probably the result of New Testament influence).

The treatment of this passage in Matthew and Luke is instructive of their different procedures and concerns. Both present a characterization of those who are as if blind and dumb (Matthew 13:13; Luke 8:10), but without immediately continuing the biblical reference. Indeed, Luke proceeds to have Jesus give the interpretation of the parable of the sower, so that what seems a clear reminiscence of the explicitly Targumic text in Mark is in the third Gospel at most a fleeting allusion. Matthew, on the other hand, attaches to the characterization a full, word for word, quotation of Isaiah 6:9, 10 in the Septuagint, prefaced with the often repeated observation in this Gospel that the passage was "fulfilled" in Jesus' ministry (Matthew 13:14, 15). In Luke, then, the reference is tenuous, while in Matthew it is spelled out, but in terms of the Greek tradition of biblical translation. Yet even though the reference seems relatively unimportant to Luke, and of primary interest to Matthew only in its Septuagintal form, their characterization of the wilfully blind and deaf is as in Mark — and the Targum — presented with the use of the third person, rather than the second. The use of the participles "hearing" and "seeing" represent further points of contact which Matthew and Luke have with Mark and the Targum. Mark's colleagues therefore seem to present much the same tradition as Mark does, but not as completely as Mark.

Although Mark presents the fullest parallel to the specifically Targumic form of Isaiah 6:9, 10, and seems to be reliant on it, his use of this material in the saying of Jesus obviously does not involve the word for word citation of the written Targumic source known to us. The reference to the idea in Isaiah 6:9, 10 is obvious, and Matthew shows that at least one tradent was quite consciously aware of this fact; further, the particular elements in the saying noted above show that the reference is closest to the Targumic rendering of Isaiah, and in the light of the contacts with the Targum, it is clear that the saying does not represent a complete or arbitrary alteration of the biblical text. Nonetheless, there is a marked departure from any known biblical text in the dominical "citation," and this phenomenon is as striking as the reliance on Targumic tradition. What purpose can this particular allusion to Isaiah possibly serve in the Markan passage? To begin on a negative note, the purpose does not seem to be that of showing that parables are told expressly so that people do not understand them. As Manson also points out (1955, p. 78), the saying omits the very words from the Targum ("Make the heart of this people dull...") which would have conveyed this message. Far more plausibly, Manson suggested the citation provides a "definition of the sort of character which prevents a man from becoming one of those to whom the secret of the kingdom is given" (1955, pp. 79, 80).

Manson further suggested that Mark misconstrued the Aramaic tradition which lay before him (1955, pp. 77, 78). The word at the beginning of verse twelve, here translated as "so that" can be used in Greek ($\H{\iota}\nu\alpha$) to introduce a purpose clause, and so mean "in order that." Manson took the term as having this meaning in Mark, and observed that the Aramaic word for "that" (ד) stands in the Targum (cf. v. 9: "go and speak to this people *that* hear indeed but do not understand"). Here, Aramaic ד means "that" in the sense of "who" or "which," but it is an extremely flexible term, and can mean "in order that" in certain contexts, so that a confusion of the sort proposed by Manson is at least theoretically possible. As a real probability, however, this suggestion cannot rate very highly. The vagaries of ד are known even to elementary students of Aramaic (and Syriac): whoever rendered the Aramaic saying from its original language into Greek (whether Mark or, as is more likely, a predecessor) certainly had more difficult constructions to contend with, and could never have succeeded if this particle, which cannot possibly mean "in order that" at this point in the Targum, proved too difficult for him correctly to understand. Moreover, the Greek term ($\H{\iota}\nu\alpha$) here rendered "in order that" by Manson need not be so translated and, in fact, at another point in the Gospel according to Mark where scripture is cited, it clearly does not bear this meaning:

> And how it is written of the son of man, so that ($\H{\iota}\nu\alpha$) he should suffer much and be despised? (9:12)

In both 4:12 and 9:12, "so that" or "that" (even "to the effect that") are better translations of ἵνα (which is also rather flexible in its meaning, if not so much as Aramaic ‫ד‬) than "in order that." This is confirmed by a variation in the Greek textual witnesses to Matthew 13:13, the parallel to Mark 4:12: some read ὅτι (Greek "that," quite unequivocally), while others have ἵνα (with the same basic meaning intended). By the time of the New Testament, ἵνα referred to result, and not only expressed purpose (cf. Burton [1966] pp. 90-95).

Nonetheless, many commentators take Mark 4:12 to refer to a purposive ambivalence on Jesus' part (cf. Pesch [1976] pp. 237-238). Their reading (as Pesch's argument shows) is not so much dependent on the use of ἵνα as on the preceding eleventh verse in Mark (cited above). Here, those apart from the Twelve are "outside"; they have no share in the mystery of the kingdom, and no real understanding of the parables (n.b. the use of the plural, even though only one parable has so far been told by Mark). Mark himself has a theory of how the parables are to be understood, which he clearly sets out using Jesus' ministry as his model:

> And with many such parables he spoke the word to them, as much as they could understand, and apart from parables he did not speak to them. Privately, though, to his own disciples, he explained everything (4:33, 34).

The idea here is certainly similar, but not identical, to what we meet in 4:10-12: there, the "mystery" belongs only to the Twelve and their circle, while here the parables have a positive, if only partial, value, which Jesus' disciples as a whole are in a position to augment (by explaining the parables to others). This more moderate statement is of a summary nature and comes at the close of the parables collection in Mark; for these reasons, it should be held better to reflect the concerns of the redactor than Mark 4:10-12 does. (It is likely, indeed, that Mark has weakened the exclusivity of 4:10 somewhat by adding "those around him" before the mention of the Twelve, cf. Grundmann [1959] p. 91). Given his perspective on how the parables are to be understood, Mark would not probably have read his own ἵνα as an introduction to a purpose clause, any more than he accepted the hard point of view expressed in v. 11 without qualification.

If Mark did not shape v. 11 in its present form, who did? One might suggest that it belongs within the same stream of tradition as 4:12, but one needs to be cautious before making such a suggestion. As already observed, 4:12 appears to be a characterization of those who refuse to see and hear, and not to reflect a deliberate banishment of the "outsiders." Further, some of the language in v. 11 seems to reflect the situation of the Church after Jesus. The kingdom is a "mystery," something to be revealed by God. This word occurs only here in the Gospels, and with a meaning influenced by the apocalyptic movement, for which "mystery" meant the disclosure of the final events which were to take place at the end of the world (cf. Bornkamm [1942] pp. 823-825). The usage of "mystery" in connection with the kingdom is certainly not a self-evident corollary of Jesus' public announcement of the kingdom, in which the ability of his hearers at least to understand his message was obviously presupposed. By itself, this observation does not compel us to conclude that the formulation is influenced by the experience of the Church after Jesus, but it does open this possibility.

The designation of those who fail to understand as "outsiders" corresponds exactly to the expression we find in the Pauline letters (cf. 1 Corinthians 5:12, 13; 1 Thessalonians 4:12, cf. Colossians 4:5) which is used to describe those who stand apart from the Church. The conception which lies behind this usage is that of a rather closed community, especially when compared to the attitude ascribed to Jesus towards those outside the circle of his disciples in Mark 9:38-40 (cf. Luke 9:49, 50). There, a more tolerant maxim, "he who is not against us is for us," is applied to an exorcist who used Jesus' name, but did not join the disciples. Even the term "parable" in Mark 4:11 seems more in accord with Hebrews 9:9, where it implies an element of esoteric meaning, than with the usage of the Gospels generally, where the emphasis is on the illustrative value and power of the parables. Indeed, Mark 4:13 has Jesus express frustration at his disciples' failure to understand the parable at issue, which presupposes that a parable is not a "riddle," which seems to be the sense of the usage in 4:11 (cf. Pesch [1976] p. 239).

These considerations lead us to the conclusion that the present form of this verse tells us more about the attitude of the early missionary Church to those who refused its message than about Jesus' view of his own parabolic teaching. The specific application of the saying to the Twelve, and its attachment to a tradition which stands under the influence of the Targum (v. 12), may be taken to suggest that the Jerusalem circle of disciples framed the version of the saying which Mark handed on (cf. Trocmé [1977]).

Mark, then, incorporated 4:11, 12 and developed from these verses and the parabolic material collected in chapter four a view of parables under which they could be partially understood by any one (4:33), but were fully set out by the disciples (4:34). The tradition he incorporated in vv. 11, 12 came to him through the Jerusalem Church, where the present v. 11 (directed towards the Twelve, cf. v. 10) had been shaped by the difficult experience of mission, an experience which led to the development of a rather exclusivist stance (reflected, for example, in Acts 2:22-24, 36, 42; 3:14, 15; 4:10; 13:46). V. 12, however, does not actually accord with this stance, in that it characterizes the refusal to hear Jesus' message rather than portraying that refusal as an absolute exclusion from "the mystery of the kingdom." The reference to the Targumic text does not include the very words which would have made this point, and in any case the looseness of the citation militates against the notion that it was initially designed to serve as a precise divine proscription of the "outsiders." These characteristics of the citation make it dubious that it was attributed to Jesus by the tradents who shaped v. 11, and rather more likely that v. 12 in the present text was already in circulation as a saying of Jesus at the time v. 11 was developed. Indeed, v. 11 can be said to offer an interpretation of v. 12 for a missionary

Church under immense pressure, just as vv. 33, 34 develop an understanding of v. 12 and Jesus' parabolic teaching as a whole for the Markan community. While the Markan community is urged by the Evangelist to learn to confess her Lord before her potential persecutors (10:29, 30) without confronting them with unnecessary provocation (cf. 9:41, with vv. 38-40, a unique combination of material among the Synoptic Gospels), the Jerusalem Church, through material such as 4:11, struggled to find a meaning in the tradition of Jesus' words for her failures in mission.

The tradition handed on in Mark 4:12, however, appears not to reflect the missionary experience of the Church. Rather, it represents a rebuke directed against hearers who are slow to grasp the message of a somewhat impatient speaker. "They are like those of whom Isaiah spoke," is the complaint, without any claim that they must be that way, or that God intends them to have such an attitude. The occasional nature of the reference to the Isaiah Targum, and the fact that an express form of citation is not used, do not accord well with the supposition that this reference represents the programmatic attitude of the tradents in the early Church who shaped v. 11; rather, they suggest that v. 12 is substantially a saying of Jesus.

He is portrayed as displaying a similar attitude in Mark 7:18 (cf. Matthew 15:16). His own disciples ask him the meaning of a "parable" (v. 17, here used in its Aramaic meaning: "proverb") about what defiles a man in v. 15 (cf. Matthew 15:11, 15), and he replies, "So, are you also without understanding? Do you not perceive...?" His annoyance seems natural in context; he has just called everyone, even the crowd, to understand (Mark 7:14; Matthew 15:10), and not even his disciples appear to get the message. The resulting rebuke — without benefit of an allusion to Isaiah — is even more direct than what we find in 4:12, and suggests (once again) that the Twelve may have been rather romantic about their own status in Jesus' thinking and that their estimate of themselves has influenced the shape of v. 11. Taking 7:18 and 4:12 together, a temperamental irascibility is manifest, directed against outsiders and insiders alike, in the face of a failure to grasp a parabolically illustrated message. We cannot, in the nature of the case, dogmatically conclude Jesus said precisely what is ascribed to him in 4:12, but neither have we a stronger explanation for the presence of these words in the Gospel than their authenticity. It would appear, on reflection, that Jesus rebuked his hearers for a dull-wittedness akin to that described in the Targum they used in their synagogues because he was frustrated by their response to his teaching, and wished to shame them into a more positive appreciation of his message.

"All those grasping a sword by a sword will perish"(Matthew 26:52). Although these proverbial words of Jesus are cited only by Matthew, their authenticity as a saying of Jesus himself is not seriously to be questioned. Their basic intention corresponds well to what are among the most distinctive elements of the sermon on the mount (Matthew 5:38-48; cf. 5:9) or the sermon on the plain (Luke 6:27-36), and the saying itself appears to be paraphrased in Revelation 13:10. In the Greek text of Matthew, the word which is the equivalent of English "by" is ἐν; according to ordinary Greek usage, the term is quite unnecessary here. One can convey the idea of the sword being used as the instrument of death in the Greek of this period by the use of the dative case alone (cf. Acts 12:2, and Lagrange [1927] p. 503). Precisely the same construction occurs in the Septuagint (cf. Ezekiel 5:12 for example) in order to render the Hebrew particle בּ (which can mean "by" or "on" or "in"); we can take this slight grammatical oddity (as Lagrange does) as a Semiticism. The usage of the verb "grasp," rather than "draw" (cf. v. 51 and normal New Testament usage), may also be taken as slightly unusual. The presence of a Semiticism in a dominical saying obviously does not prove it is authentic. A Semiticism may reflect the ultimately Palestinian origin of some version of the tradition preserved by an Evangelist, but not of the actual wording presented. Further, a general Semiticism is not necessarily an Aramaism; in the present case, the use of the particle בּ is ubiquitous among Semitic languages. It has been suggested recently (Turner [1976] pp.

5-10) that a Semitic type of Greek may have been used in early Christian communities as a matter of course, and not only originally Semitic traditions were handed down (cf. the linguistic peculiarities of the Revelation). Finally, as we found in our study of Mark 4:11, a saying may reflect Palestinian tradition which reflects the experience of Jesus' followers better than his own concerns.

In his monograph, entitled *The Use of the Old Testament in St. Matthew's Gospel*, Robert H. Gundry observes that Matthew 26:52 is an allusive quotation of the Isaiah Targum 50:11 (1967, pp. 144, 150). In fact, when we turn to the Targum, we find all of the primary elements which are included in Jesus' saying (here italicized):

> Behold, *all* you kindling a fire, *grasping a sword*, go, fall in the fire you kindled and *on the sword* you grasped. This is yours from my word: you shall return to your *destruction*.

Except for the word "all," each of the italicized words is unique to the Targum among Old Testament versions. "Grasping a sword" corresponds exactly to the wording and syntax of the dominical saying, and "on the sword" includes precisely the particle (ב, here rendered "on") which presumably stands behind "by" (ἐν) in the Greek text of Matthew. Only an unusual noun for "destruction," rather than a verbal form for "being destroyed" or "perishing" (Matthew's ἀπολοῦνται can be said to bear either meaning) is used, so that Jesus' reference to the Targumic tradition must be characterized as paraphrastic as well as radically abbreviated. Nonetheless, Gundry's point (based on the discovery of the parallel by H. Kosmala [1960]) is striking and its importance should not be overlooked.

The relationship between this saying and the Isaiah Targum is much as we found in the case of Mark 4:12. The coherence with the Aramaic version seems clear, and yet the dominical sayings are much shorter than the Targumic texts, and are possessed of a markedly independent element. One might infer from this that Jesus cited a more primitive

Targum whose wording was similar to, but different from, that of the Targum to which we have access. An element of change in the Targumic tradition before 70 A.D. should certainly be allowed for, since its evolution after 70 A.D.— when rabbinic control was more complete, and therefore change presumably more difficult to come by—has been established (cf. part one of the present volume). This implies that what might only seem to us a partial or shadowy reference to the Isaian text may have been a rather more exact quotation to the ears of Jesus' first audience. On the other hand, the radical brevity of the sayings as compared to any known version of the Isaian text should warn us away from trying to explain all of Jesus' deviations from the Targum on the basis of changes in the Targumic tradition. It is far more likely that a characteristic of his style of preaching was to vivify his message by the use of language and imagery taken from the translation tradition of the synagogues of his day without full or extensive citation.

The incomplete usage of the Targum can be taken as another indication that this saying was, much as we have it, spoken by Jesus. When the Evangelists reverted to the version of scripture best known to them and revered in their communities (the Septuagint), they cited it extensively, not partially or in the sporadic fashion we have seen instanced in two dominical sayings. This observation tells against Gundry's extreme thesis — which has perhaps prevented his study from receiving the attention it deserves — that Matthew, an immediate follower of Jesus, was trilingual (speaking Hebrew, Aramaic and Greek) and so took notes in three languages and cited the Bible in three versions (1967, p. 183, but cf. p. 89). Such theses appear to be desperate expedients to avoid the recognition that traditions about Jesus in the New Testament underwent development as they were passed on by word of mouth and later in writing. This process involved changes, not only of language and biblical versions, but also of theology (as we saw in the case of Mark 4:11, 12 and have observed in connection with Matthew's accounts of Jesus' first public preaching, the Canaanite woman's request, and the death of Jesus). To ascribe all such alterations to the Evangelists individually — no matter how talented, educated and many-faceted they are imagined to be — seems more a dogmatic than a critical judgment. Moreover, Gundry's thesis easily leads one to ignore the very indications that Jesus himself said what Matthew 26:52 says he did. Unlike the Matthean citations of the Old Testament which follow the Septuagint, and unlike those which reflect a tradition departing from the Septuagint to some extent (partially in the direction of the Hebrew text), this verse joins the very few in the first Gospel which manifest a very different handling of scripture. Here it is not quoted verbatim, but used to make a specific point within the concrete context of Jesus' ministry. The lack of extensive citation of the biblical tradition, and of an evident theological context in the experience of the Church, which corresponds to the interests of the saying, are further indications, along with its coherence with the Isaiah Targum and Jesus' attitude towards violence as reflected elsewhere in the Synoptic tradition, that Matthew 26:52 is in fact a saying of Jesus.

In Mark 9:48 Jesus is presented as describing "Gehenna" (cf. v. 47) as the place "where their worm does not die and the fire is not quenched." This is a generally literal rendering of Isaiah 66:24b, except for the use of the present tense (instead of the future). The Targum is much more paraphrastic at this point, reading "for their souls will not die, and their fire will not be quenched." The Septuagint, on the other hand, represents the Hebrew text very exactly: "for their worm will not die, and their fire will not be quenched." Mark has "where" instead of "for," and he omits the second use of "their," so that there is fairly close, but far from exact, verbal agreement with the Septuagint.

In fact, however, the omission of the second "their," the use of "where" and the tense change correspond to and reflect the very purpose of the citation in its present context: it is a description of Gehenna, the valley to the south of Jerusalem which was thought to be the appointed site of the final judgment (cf. Jeremias [1933] p. 655). As such, it is indeed a specific place "where" punishment occurs, and the fire is not merely "their" fire, but an objective reality. The alteration in tenses is also accounted for by the use of the citation in order to describe Gehenna vividly and to make its threat more concrete.

This passage is frequently connected with Gehenna in rabbinic literature from the time of the ascription by Mishnah ('Eduyoth 2:10) to Rabbi Aqiba of the view that Isaiah 66:23f. describes the punishment of the wicked. (Further examples are given in Strack-Billerbeck [1924] p. 20.) The connection with Gehenna (Aramaic: Gehinnam) as attested in the Targum, however, brings us closer chronologically to the New Testament than the rest of Rabbinica, and instances the general proclivity of the Targumic interpreters to speak of the punishment that awaits the wicked in the appointed valley (cf. 26:15, 19; 30:33; 33:14, 17; 53:9; 65:5). Such frequent reference to Gehenna, occasioned by the biblical text, is the probable background of the connection of Isaiah 66:24 to the mention of Gehenna in Mark 9:47, 48, and in this regard also the Targum presents a closer analogy to the dominical saying than the Mishnah.

The saying of Jesus, whose essential authenticity seems assured (cf. Lagrange [1929] p. 252; Lane [1974] p. 347f.), is obviously quite comprehensible without reference to the Targum. But his reference to Isaiah 66:24 in connection with Gehenna, as if it were self-evidently relevant, does require explanation. Moreover, many New Testament manuscripts also give Isaiah 66:24 in the form in which it appears in v. 48 at v. 44 and v. 46, so that the reference becomes a refrain through the entire passage (vv. 43-48) which attaches to every mention of Gehenna. (Vv. 44 and 46 are not included at all in many important manuscripts.) Whether we take this variant reading as the intended text of Mark, or as a refrain which was added at some other point in the course of the transmission of this series of sayings, the fact remains that its very existence presupposes the clear understanding that Gehenna is to be taken in the sense of what is described in Isaiah 66:24.

Certain possibilities immediately spring to mind as explanations of the fact that some manuscripts read vv. 44, 46 and some do not. Jesus might well have repeated the citation; once the sayings left the circle in which the Targumic allusion would have been appreciated, this repetition would have appeared pointless, and therefore all but one citation superfluous. Equally, an early tradent of the sayings who spotted the allusion may have made v. 48 into a refrain by repeating it (vv. 44, 46), or Mark may have done the same thing on the basis of the recognition of a Septuagintal allusion. Finally, as most modern editors of the New Testament believe, the repetition might reflect the theology of later scribes (presumably also based on the recognition of an allusion to the Septuagint) who copied the text of Mark. In two verses of the Septuagint (Ecclesiasticus 7:17 and Judith 16:17) fire and worm imagery, perhaps reminiscent of Isaiah 66:24, is used in the context of judgment, and this might help to explain why a tradent of the Jesus saying (be he Mark, a predecessor or successor) to whom the Septuagint was the standard version of scripture might have made the citation into a refrain. But neither of the passages is anything like a citation of Isaiah (cf. Schmid [1954] p. 183), so that this argument is less than convincing. More to the point, the Septuagintal usages do not explain, as the Targumic usage does, why anyone (Jesus or one of his followers) would have associated Isaiah 66:24 with Gehenna.

The last observation is reinforced when we consider the other references to Gehenna in the New Testament. Except for James 3:6, the usage of the word Gehenna ($\gamma\acute{\epsilon}\epsilon\nu\nu\alpha$) is limited to sayings of Jesus (aside from Mark 9:43, 45, 47, cf. Matthew 5:22, 29, 30; 10:28; 18:9; 23:15, 33; Luke 12:5). The treatment of sayings which include the term by Mark's colleagues is indicative of their attitude to the concept of Gehenna, to which they made reference more out of respect for the Jesus tradition than out of enthusiasm for the idea.

In 5:22, the first usage of $\gamma\acute{\epsilon}\epsilon\nu\nu\alpha$ in his Gospel, Matthew adds "of fire" to the term in order to make its meaning clearer. In vv. 29 and 30 of the same chapter, no such qualification is necessary, because the concept has already been introduced with its explanatory qualification. The order of the sayings therefore seems to reflect a conscious

plan of presentation, and it is also remarkable that v. 29 (the
eye saying) parallels Mark 9:47 while v. 30 (the hand saying)
parallels Mark 9:43, which raises the possibility that Matthew has altered the order of the sayings in the tradition
before him. Both sayings are given in Matthew under the
heading of adultery (cf. Matthew 5:27) and serve to underline the statement that whoever looks at a woman desirously
has already committed adultery with her in his heart. The
relevance of v. 30 to this is far from perfect, and some
manuscripts in fact omit the verse. While these considerations do not prove that Matthew actually used the text of
Mark, they do support the contention that the literary
structure of the antitheses in the sermon on the mount in
Matthew (sayings material of the type, "You have heard that
it was said.... But I say to you...") is artificial, and that
Mark in this instance presents a purer form of the sort of
tradition incorporated by Matthew (cf. Grundmann [1971]
p. 159). Matthew in fact presents a second parallel to Mark
9:43 in chapter eighteen, along with a second parallel to
Mark 9:47 (cf. Matthew 18:8, 9). The context of these
parallels is, as in Mark chapter nine, that of causing the least
believer to stumble (cf. Matthew 18:6; Mark 9:42), and not
that of adultery. In 18:8, however, Matthew has Jesus refer,
not to Gehenna, but to "eternal fire." This corresponds to
the qualification of "Gehenna" with "of fire" in 5:22, a usage
which appears again in 18:9. Matthew therefore betrays his
knowledge of Gehenna sayings such as we have in Mark
9:42-48, and he consistently presents a more interpreted
form of this material than Mark does. The remaining
Gehenna sayings in Matthew (10:28; 23:15, 33) show, however, that he does have access to primitive tradition which
Mark does not present (cf. Strack-Billerbeck [1926] pp.
580-581, 924-931, 940).

Luke presents only one Gehenna saying (Luke 12:5),
which is a parallel to Matthew 10:28. The evident tendency
of Matthew, therefore, is to interpret Gehenna sayings in
terms of an eternal fire of punishment, while Luke — consciously or not — restricts the number of such sayings
severely. Basically, therefore, the Markan version of Jesus'

sayings about Gehenna and scandal (9:42-48) seems to be the earliest in the Synoptic tradition. We cannot know whether the traditions before Matthew and Luke ever contained a reference to Isaiah 66:24, which is not included in the extant texts, but their omission (again, deliberate or not) of the citation is consistent with our suggestion that its association with Gehenna presupposes the Targumic interpretation, familiarity with which declined as the Gospel tradition developed. Moreover, the omission of the citation in Matthew and especially in Luke (to whom the Septuagint was practically speaking the normative version of scripture) tells against the supposition that it would have been valued in a circle familiar with the Septuagintal Ecclesiasticus 7:17 and Judith 16:17. Against the background of the development of Gehenna sayings in the Synoptic tradition, Mark 9:44, 46, 48 stand out as reflecting the Targumic interpretation of Isaiah 66:24.

In view of these considerations, Mark 9:44, 46 — whose attestation textually is in any case both wide and early —should perhaps be looked at again as belonging properly to the text of the Gospel. Their omission is, as suggested above, fairly easily accounted for on the understanding that, as the sayings tradition entered a more Hellenistic, less Jewish and Aramaic environment, the Targumic associations of the citation were lost. Consequently, the hypothesis that the citation in v. 48 and the refrain texts (vv. 44, 46) belong to an originally Aramaic stream of the Synoptic tradition appears tenable. But the inclusion of all three citations lends to Mark 9:42-48 an almost liturgical tone, and such a repetition of a biblical text is not elsewhere a characteristic of Jesus' teaching in Mark's Gospel. Vv. 44, 46, therefore, seem to represent the awareness of the importance of the biblical citation to Jesus' teaching on Gehenna by tradents of his sayings, sensitive to the Targumic background of his message, who emphasized the citation by repeating it. The omission of the repetitive material by Mark or later scribes reflects how odd it sounded to those who were unfamiliar with the Targumic application of Isaiah 66:24, and who perhaps knew very well that it was not

Jesus' habit to teach using a biblical text as a refrain in this manner. The eventual omission of the refrain in the course of the post-Aramaic transmission of vv. 42-48 is therefore explicable, while its secondary inclusion in a Greek-speaking context is anomalous. On balance, the oddity of vv. 44, 46 within the Markan presentation of Jesus' teaching would favour the view that Mark did not include these verses, while their attestation in some manuscripts may reflect the originally Aramaic tradition on which Mark was dependent. Such a solution permits us to do justice both to the wide textual attestation of the omission of the two unusual verses, and to the affinity with the Targumic interpretation which is manifest in them.

The repetition of v. 48 in vv. 44, 46 would appear, then, to reflect an acknowledgement and appreciation of Jesus' citation of Isaiah 66:24 in his teaching on Gehenna. The fact that v. 48 is not an exact quotation of the verse from Isaiah in any ancient version, however, tells against the supposition that "where their worm does not die and the fire is not quenched" was originally designed to serve as an exact biblical refrain within this teaching. The unanimously attested v. 48 should rather be taken as the fundamental usage, pertinent to Gehenna in view of the Targumic interpretation of Isaiah 66:24, which was repeated by tradents who appreciated the significance of this usage. The repetition would also, of course, make this speech easier to memorize and pass on to Christian groups for their instruction.

The inexact nature of the biblical citation in v. 48 itself reminds us of our findings in respect of Mark 4:12 and Matthew 26:52. One might begin to discern a characteristic of Jesus' use of Targumic interpretation, namely that he referred to it without precise citation. The exact citation of the Septuagint would have suited Mark better, and an exact citation of the Targum would have suited the pre-Markan tradents who added vv. 44, 46 to the speech. Again, of course, we must be careful with such arguments, since we do not have direct access to the Greek or Aramaic renderings which were current in the first century. Nonetheless, the distinctive elements in v. 48 ("where," the tense change, the omission of the second "their") make it appear to represent a consistent view of Isaiah 66:24 which no ancient version of Isaiah exactly reflects (although the Targumic connection with Gehenna appears to reflect its point of departure). The nature of the reference therefore presupposes its origin before Mark, and before Mark's predecessors. The redaction history and tradition history of Mark 9:48 are consistent with the notion that it represents Jesus' thinking on Gehenna, and — in the absence of evidence that the form of citation was influenced by the concerns of the Church rather than those of Jesus — the substantive authenticity of the verse best accounts for its presence in Mark.

A1 FINDINGS

Before proceeding to our next category of coherence between the Isaiah Targum and sayings of Jesus, it would perhaps clarify our progress to this point if we reviewed our findings. The verbal agreements between Mark 4:12 and Targum Isaiah 6:9, 10 and (albeit to a lesser extent) between Matthew 26:52 and Targum Isaiah 50:11, agreements which are not explicable in respect of other ancient versions of the Old Testament, led us to conclude in each case that the Targumic interpretation provided the background of the dominical saying. Verbal agreement between Mark 9:48 and Targum Isaiah 66:24 was also apparent, but not in a degree which by itself would reasonably lead to the conclusion that the Targum sheds light on the background of the saying. But the use of the term "Gehenna" in Mark 9:47 corresponds to the appearance of "Gehinnam" in the Targumic text, and the association between Gehenna and Isaiah 66:24 seemed under analysis to constitute the presupposition of the saying. (One might take the Gehenna material to be more a thematic than a dictional correspondence, in which case one would treat it under our category "B1." On the other hand, "Gehinnam" expressly appears in the Targumic text, and Mark 9:48 is strictly and immediately related to the reference to "Gehenna" in v. 47 by the introductory and innovative use of the term "where," so that the categorization of this coherence under "A1" seems preferable.) In all three instances, therefore, dictional coherence (as described in the introduction to part two) between the sayings and the Targum has been established.

The discovery of these correspondences has, in turn, permitted us to set the transmission of the sayings in a fresh light. Mark 4:12 appeared to be a characterization of Jesus' hearers in biblical (that is to say, Targumic) terms which expressed frustration at their sluggish response and demanded something better. The reshaping and reinterpretation of this saying in the early Church became evident in Mark 4:11, where the exclusive understanding of Jesus' message is claimed for the Twelve and their associates. Mark himself, finally, seems to have taken this rather stark position as an indication that the meaning of the parables is available generally only through Jesus' followers as a whole (4:33, 34). Matthew 26:52, commonly regarded as authentically dominical, is now, with its Targumic background, provided with a tradition history which is consistent with that judgment. Mark 9:48, despite its at first sight Septuagintal rendering of Isaiah 66:24, is seen to proceed from the Targumic understanding of the Isaian text, and the Targumic association between "Gehinnam" and Isaiah 66:24 also provided us with the necessary evidence to explain that the repetition of the citation at vv. 44, 46 in some manuscripts represents the influence of an early, but secondary, development of Jesus' teaching about Gehenna.

Dictional coherence with the Targum and the tradition history of the sayings have also provided us with indications which, along with others, suggest that the sayings (with the notable exception of Mark 4:11) are actually sayings of Jesus. By itself, this might be taken as a sufficiently interesting finding to warrant the observation of these connections with the Targum; in fact, however, such observation illuminates not only the authenticity, but also the meaning, of the sayings. Mark 4:12 shows itself as a scornful comment on dull-witted listeners, not Jesus' articulation of a programmatic attempt to mislead his hearers with parables. If we did not appreciate the Targumic background of Matthew 26:52, it might seem to us — in its present context — a sententious maxim uttered in circumstances so trying that it would likely confuse the disciples. But understood as a reminder of the Isaian paraphrase the disciples were familiar with from synagogue worship, the saying appears as a call for an attitude the disciples should already have maintained, and therefore as a more readily understandable reprimand. Similarly, the association of Isaiah 66:24 with Jesus' speech about Gehenna in Mark 9:48 is now to be understood more as a substantiation, through the Targumic understanding of the verse, of the picture of destruction which Jesus evokes than as a creative attempt to provide the teaching with a proof text from scripture.

The development, authenticity and meaning of three dominical sayings has, therefore, been illuminated with reference to their correspondences with the Isaiah Targum. (Other observations and methods of argument have, of course, also been employed, but these correspondences have provided the focus of our discussion.) At the same time, a pattern of Jesus' usage of the Targumic interpretation is beginning to emerge. In each case, Jesus does not — in the strictest sense — cite the Targum: Isaiah is not explicitly named in any of the sayings (cf. Mark 7:6, and the parallels). And although Mark 4:12 and 9:48 might just be called "quotations" of the Targum, using the term loosely, they hardly amount to literal renderings of the Aramaic text, or any known ancient text, of Isaiah, and Matthew 26:52 can scarcely be called a "citation" of the Targum on even the loosest understanding of the word. Nonetheless, in all three cases the coherence with Targumic diction seems to justify the observation that Jesus refers to the Targumic tradition in his preaching. Following the practice of recent studies of the use of the Old Testament in the New Testament, one may speak of such references as citations, quotations or allusions, but only to suggest the relative proximity of a given saying to the Targumic text in comparison with others, and (obviously) on the understanding that none of the sayings literally cites, quotes, alludes to or uses the Targumic *text*, which did not begin to emerge until some forty years after

Jesus' death. Even the verb "refer" and the noun "reference" could be taken in a misleading way, since we commonly say that a given writer refers or makes reference to a particular literary source (for example in a footnote). The point is that the cultural distance between the literate readers of this study and the semi-literate hearers of Jesus forces us to describe Jesus' "reference" to his "sources" (yet another potentially misleading word!) with language which is strictly speaking inaccurate. We must use such language in a transferred sense in order to speak at all, but we must also bear in mind that we can only use it in that way, without treating our own descriptions as a reason for believing that every "source" which is "cited," "quoted," "alluded to" or otherwise "used" is necessarily a written document. Speaking distributively, then, Jesus refers to the Targum in order to enliven his message. Those who fail to take his meaning are compared to Isaiah's sluggish contemporaries; the disciples are called to remember the warning against armed violence in the Targum as Jesus is arrested; Gehenna is said to be just as desolating as the Targum says it is.

As has already been suggested, we might discover that Jesus' references to the Targum were a bit more precise if we had direct access today to the Targumic interpretation of his time. In the instances of each of the three sayings discussed, however, we have observed such a dramatic departure from any known text of Isaiah as to compel the observation that there is a richly creative element in Jesus' use of Targumic tradition. Just this point, incidentally, also makes it evident that the Targumic passages discussed have not been influenced by the tradition of Jesus' sayings. It is perhaps unlikely in general that the positive influence of New Testament teaching was exerted on the Targum, but one cannot exclude the possibility absolutely. The evidence so far considered, however, lends no support to this theoretical possibility. The Targumic passages also are not patient of the understanding that the New Testament is a negative influence: that is, there is no indication in them that Jesus' sayings are being refuted. Jesus, in a word, seems to have used Targumic interpretation without limiting himself to it.

The way he used Targumic tradition is obviously of significance for appreciating how he understood the Old Testament and applied it in his teaching, but this question can only be approached after more evidence has been considered.

B1 INSTANCES OF THEMATIC COHERENCE WITH THE TARGUM IN DOMINICAL REFERENCES TO ISAIAH

Each of the Synoptic Gospels presents a parable after the report of Jesus' occupation of the Temple (Matthew 21·33-46; Mark 12:1-12; Luke 20:9-19). The parable as a whole tells of a man who plants and prepares a vineyard, lets it out to tenants and departs in the expectation that he will be able to send servants to acquire his share of the proceeds. But a succession of his delegates are abused; even his son is killed. In these circumstances it is said the owner will punish the tenants and hire out his vineyard to others. The parable closes with the words, "The stone which the builders rejected...," a citation of Psalm 118:22-23 (except in Luke, where only v. 22 is cited), followed by the notice that Jesus' opponents sought to arrest him (Matthew 21:42-46; Mark 12:10-12; Luke 20:17-19).

The vivid vineyard imagery found in Isaiah 5:1-7 seems to be the starting point of the parable; there, too, the vineyard is a figure for Israel in the context of judgment, and God is pictured as preparing the vineyard and expecting a return. Particularly, Matthew (21:33) and Mark (12:1) allude to Isaiah 5:2 in setting the scene of the parable (cf. Hill [1972] p. 299 and Anderson [1976] p. 272) and, as we have grown to expect from these Greek-speaking Evangelists, their allusion corresponds better to the Septuagint than to the Targum or the Masoretic text. They speak of a hedge set around the vineyard, which reference is found only in the Septuagint, and their choice of words corresponds generally to that of the Greek version at this point. That the third person is used in the parable instead of the first person, however, is but the most significant example of the departure of its language from any known text of Isaiah, a departure which prevents us from calling the parable a quotation or citation of the biblical imagery. Given that Isaiah provides the starting point of the parable, it obviously proceeds in a very original way. Yet the Evangelists agree that the Jewish leaders immediately take action, understanding that the parable is directed against them. Incidentally, this notice conflicts with the idea that Jesus' parables were deliberately made obscure to "outsiders" (cf. above on Mark 4:11-12). The leaders concerned are chief priests, scribes and elders (Mark 12:12, referring back to 11:27), or chief priests and Pharisees (Matthew 21:45), or scribes and chief priests (Luke 20:19): how is it that they take the parable as applying to themselves, while the Isaian passage which is its premise refers to the house of Israel, or more particularly to Judah (cf. vv. 3, 7)? The context of the passage in the Temple controversy provides at least a partial explanation, but the interpretation found in the Targum suggests that the parable would be understood in this way even apart from its present literary context. In the Targum, v. 2 of the fifth chapter of Isaiah refers to the sanctuary and the altar as part of God's preparation of the vineyard. If this represents the understanding of this imagery at the time the parable was first told, it would explain why it was taken to refer principally to those associated with the maintenance of the Temple cult.

Our observation does not apply to the Targumic passage as a whole, however, because reference is also made there to the removal of God's presence (Shekhinah) from Jerusalem, plunder, desolation, the destruction of "sanctuaries" (probably synagogues), exile and forsakenness (vv. 5, 6): these elements appear to be part of the vivid recollection of an interpreter who remembered the outcome of the successful Roman siege under Vespasian and Titus. None of these elements, however, is as specifically cultic as the reading in v. 2, which agrees with the interpretation of this verse by a Tannaitic rabbi (Jose, whose view is given in Sukkah 49a) in a dictum which does not refer to the destruction of the Temple. The rabbi by no means antedates this event, but his opinion indicates that a cultic interpretation of v. 2 was not necessarily tied to a reference or allusion to the destruction of the Temple. In fact, several terms are used in connection with the interpretation of v. 2 in the Targum ("Abraham," "house of Israel," "law," "repent" in vv. 1, 3) which are characteristic of its earlier framework as isolated in part one of the present study. The possibility does seem strong, therefore, that the parable, contexted in Temple controversy and directed against the Temple leadership, reflects the specifically cultic context of Isaiah 5:1-7 in the Targum.

The thematic coherence between the Targum and the parable therefore helps to explain the placement and meaning of the latter. Particularly, the immediate understanding of the parable by Jesus' opponents is more explicable than it would be otherwise on the supposition that they took the imagery in terms of the Targumic interpretation. Since the context and point of the parable are quite consistent throughout the Synoptic Gospels, despite minor variations of placement and wording, no single Evangelist is likely responsible for the coherence with the Targum. Indeed, the evident allusion to the Septuagint in the Matthean and Markan texts suggests that we must look to the tradition before the Evangelists for the origin of this coherence.

In his recent commentary on Luke's Gospel, I. Howard Marshall observes that, in contemporary research, two seemingly contradictory findings have been confirmed. The economic relationships portrayed in the parable accord with Palestinian custom, and yet the place and fate of the son in the parable can be taken, and may be intended, allegorically to speak of Jesus (1978, pp. 726-727). Marshall himself argues that the parable was told by Jesus but developed allegorically as it was transmitted, and in fact the explicit use of Psalm 118 is not found in the parallel in *The Gospel according to Thomas* (saying 65), and the Lukan version of the parable does not present the rejection of God's messengers by Israel's leaders as dramatically as the Markan and (especially the) Matthean versions do (cf. Grundmann [1971] pp. 460-461). A position such as Marshall's would do justice to the two tendencies in recent research which he calls attention to, and help to explain the tension between the thematic coherence with the Targum and the dictional coherence with the Septuagint. The difficulty with Marshall's judgment, however, is that he can offer no account of a base tradition which provided the occasion for the allegorical growth. Our investigation would suggest that the basis of the parable is a complaint about the Temple leadership, an element which the Evangelists convey only by the literary context they provide, but which was immediately obvious to Jesus' first hearers, because they understood his imagery in terms of the Targumic rendering of Isaiah. That Jesus engaged in controversy with the Temple authorities is well known, and there is also other material from the Synoptic tradition which indicates he especially attacked them for their treatment — if only indirectly — of the prophets (cf. Luke 11:47-51; 13:34a; Matthew 23:29-37a). On the other hand, the evident emphasis in the parable as it stands is not on the treatment of the prophets by the leaders, but on their treatment of Jesus as the son. Even the observation that he is cast out of the vineyard (Matthew 21:39; Mark 12:8; Luke 20:15) corresponds better to New Testament descriptions of and reflections on Jesus' death after the fact (cf. Hebrews 13:13 with Matthew 27:33; Mark 15:22; Luke 23:33, which place the crucifixion outside of Jerusalem proper) than to any saying actually attributed to Jesus. The focus on the guilt of the leaders in Jesus' death is also reminiscent of the assertions of the apostles in Acts (cf. 2:23, 36, 3:14, 15; 4:10). The present Synoptic texts seem to reflect both a dominical parable whose emphasis fell unmistakably (against its Targumic background) on the guilt of the cultic authorities in the treatment of the prophets and the development of that parable by Jesus' followers after his crucifixion in order to take account of his death.

B1 FINDINGS

The single instance of coherence we have offered in this section supports our findings in respect of the three instances treated under section "A1." Although the reference to the Targumic interpretation seems clear, there is here also no question of an exact quotation, nor is the imagery of the biblical passage as a whole taken up exactly. This observation applies both to the dominical parable, which relates to the treatment of the prophets by Israel's cultic leadership, and to its embellishment by Jesus' followers in order to apply to his death. Reflection on the Targumic antecedents of Jesus' preaching has therefore again proved to help in the distinction between what Jesus actually said and how his followers applied what he said. At the same time, even the dominical usage of the Targumic interpretation, which was closer to the Targum as we know it than the parable his followers developed and the Evangelists handed on, was innovative in its attacking posture, a posture which the Targum of Jesus' own day did not likely reflect.

The present instance also joins the previous three in that the observation of the Targumic antecedent helps us better to understand the meaning of the dominical saying: its express relevance for the Temple authorities is more readily appreciated. The question does emerge, however, whether Jesus' hearers would actually have identified references to the Targumic interpretation of Isaiah consciously. In the present case, we have posited a conscious awareness on the part of Jesus' opponents that he appealed to the application of the vineyard imagery of Isaiah 5 to the Temple in the Targumic tradition, and on that basis turned this image into an attack on them as murderers of the prophets. Notably, all of the Evangelists ascribe an understanding of the parable only to Jesus' opponents, as if a degree of sophistication were necessary in order to grasp its message. This situation is qualitatively different from what we have seen in the previous section, where the dominical sayings were directed to Jesus' followers (on one occasion [Mark 9:48] in a rather general way) under the assumption they would be readily understood. Moreover, the previous three sayings involve the use of openly employed Targumic language, while the present parable invokes the Targumic interpretation without warning. In the first cases, although we can usefully

observe the Targumic antecedents in order to distinguish
Jesus' message from his followers' development of his message, and in order to avoid misleading interpretations which
only appeal to us because we do not naturally have an
appreciation for the context of his preaching (cf. Mark 4:12
especially), his first hearers could presumably have understood him without consciously identifying his use of the
Targumic tradition of the time. For them, Jesus' use of
Targumic language might simply have enhanced the authority of his words, much as a preacher today might underline
his theme by putting it in terms reminiscent of a well known
translation of the Bible. In the present case, however, Jesus
is able to point the parable of the vineyard against the
Temple authorities precisely because he plays on their conscious familiarity with Jewish (in this case Targumic) tradition. His first hearers were probably not all cognizant of the
Targumic antecedents of his teaching, but Jesus himself
seems to have been well aware of them. He does not seem,
however, usually to have assumed an express knowledge of
the Targumic interpretation on the part of his hearers; the
present parable stands out as the single recorded instance in
which Jesus consciously shaped a saying so that only those
familiar with the Isaiah Targum of the time could fully and
readily understand it.

A2 INSTANCES OF DICTIONAL COHERENCE WITH THE TARGUM IN OTHER DOMINICAL SAYINGS

We have so far seen that Jesus appears clearly to have
used language at least partially preserved in the extant
Targum to Isaiah in contexts in which a reference to the
biblical book is implied. But his use of such language was
not generally designed to limit the understanding of his
message to those who had a specialist knowledge of the
Targumic tradition. At this stage, it must be remembered,
the Isaiah Targum was not a document, but an assortment
of local translations which were eventually incorporated
into a complete translation of Isaiah, a translation of which

the written document we possess is a developed form. A measure of agreement between these various traditions of translation must already have existed in the time of Jesus, since it was possible for their formal consolidation to begin shortly before 70 A.D. Moreover, Jesus' appeal to Targumic language and imagery presupposes a degree of familiarity on the part of his hearers with a tradition such as the Targum itself reflects. Nonetheless, we must not imagine that there was a single Targumic interpretation in respect of Isaiah, nor that every Jew in Palestine was necessarily able to recite the Isaiah Targum of his own community verbatim. At most, we might reasonably expect that pious male members of a given community could with some practice deliver a targum for those Isaian passages which were read in their synagogue. As we have already suggested, Jesus used the Targumic interpretation of Isaiah more to colour his message than to define it: one could have understood his message without recourse to this tradition for the most part, although one would probably have missed a great deal of the impact it was intended to have if one had no awareness of its background.

If, as the case seems to be, Jesus did not use the Targumic interpretation of Isaiah programmatically, but simply in order to colour his message and express the authority he believed it had, then it is quite possible that he used its language even when he did not specifically refer to the Bible, in the ordinary conduct of his preaching. The present section is devoted to just such cases, where the agreement between the Targum and the dominical saying is striking, even though Jesus is not portrayed in the saying as referring specifically to the book of Isaiah.

In the Hebrew text of Isaiah 5:23 a woe is pronounced against "those acquitting the wicked for a bribe," which the Septuagint renders, "those acquitting the impious for the sake of gifts." The Targum essentially agrees with the Hebrew and Greek versions, but has the phrase "mammon of deceit" for "bribe" or "gift" (cf. also Targum Isaiah 33:15). "Mammon" by itself, of course, is the Aramaic term for "money," and is used without qualification in the famous saying, "You cannot serve God and mammon" (Matthew 6:24; Luke 16:13). At the end of the parable of the crafty steward (Luke 16:1-8), we find the saying appended, "Make yourselves friends from the mammon of injustice" (16:9). "Mammon" here is qualified, and refers in context to the sort of bribery the crafty steward practised with his master's customers in order to better his prospects. The phrase "mammon of injustice" is clumsy in Greek; "unjust mammon" — as in fact appears in Luke 16:11 and in one Greek manuscript at v. 9 itself — would be far more natural. In Semitic languages, the qualification of one noun by another is characteristic, so that the possibility that there is some connection between the diction of the Targum and that of the dominical saying which explains their similarity in meaning cannot be ruled out.

The phrase "mammon of deceit" also appears in rabbinic literature in order to refer to dishonest gain, which indicates that mammon in itself was not felt to be necessarily wicked (cf. Strack — Billerbeck [1924] p. 220). Howard Marshall observes that "mammon of injustice" in Luke is a more globally pejorative characterization than suits the rabbinic usage, and he suggests, following Hans Kosmala (1964), that the Qumran phrase "wealth of wickedness" is a better parallel (1978, p. 621). There are, however, difficulties with this point of view. First, the "wealth" (הון) of which the scrolls speak sounds quite unlike Aramaic "mammon" (ממון), and the latter term is actually used in the famous saying of Jesus cited above as well as in Luke 16:9. Second, "wealth of wickedness" refers specifically to what should not be used for gain or enjoyment because it belongs to the realm of the sanctuary; its employment for a non-cultic purpose would constitute defilement (cf. Ginzberg [1976] p. 31; Murphy-O'Connor [1971] p. 219). For both reasons, the Qumran parallel does not seem to be more striking than the rabbinic parallel. Marshall's caution about the latter is nonetheless completely appropriate, because mammon by itself seems to have a negative connotation in the Gospel tradition which it does not consistently have in rabbinic tradition, and because "mammon of injustice" is a more damning phrase than the rabbinic "mammon of deceit," which essentially refers to dishonest acquisition, not to intrinsically suspect wealth.

As already observed, however, the immediate context of Luke 16:9 would suggest that "mammon of injustice" has to do with bribery, which is what "mammon of deceit" refers to in the Targum. The question is: should we read v. 9 as the close of the parable, or is the connection of the saying to the parable a later development which occurred in the course of the transmission of Jesus's teaching (cf. Marshall[1978] pp. 616-622; Grundman [1969] pp. 319-321)? The reference to the "money-loving" Pharisees in a narrative sentence (v. 14) at the end of a series of statements relating to wealth which begins with v. 9 would suggest that Luke was interested in developing the theme of the basic wickedness of wealth, which was dear to him (cf. Degenhardt [1965]). Moreover, the sayings in vv. 10-13 would seem to have had a different original context, because they demand faithfulness with (vv. 10-12) or abstention from (v. 13) mammon, not the sort of cleverness the parable illustrates and commends. These sayings may well have been contexted here because they include the use of the term "mammon" in vv. 11, 13. (The use of the adjective "unjust" in v. 11 was, in turn, probably designed to strengthen the link of the saying with v. 9.) This implies, however, that there was an original "mammon" saying which vv. 10-13 could be ordered around, and v. 9 suits its present context: the disciples, just as the steward in the parable, are called in this verse to use every means — even purchasing heavenly friendship at the price of wealth to which they have no right — to put themselves in a better position when the present order passes away.

Indeed, v. 9 gives the necessary clue as to the meaning of this strange parable. In the story of the crafty steward, the situation of the believer is portrayed in the bleakest of terms: he is, by rights, to be fired because he has squandered what is not really his (vv. 1, 2). Desperate for friendship (vv. 3, 4), he offers bribes of his master's wealth in order to secure his position when his job will no longer support him (vv. 5-7). Incredibly, the master (literally, "the lord"[cf. v. 1], wording which prepares us for something which reflects God's attitude more than that of wealthy people in general [cf. Marshall (1978) pp. 619-620]), praises the steward's "injustice because he acted cleverly" (v. 8). The parable shows clearly that Jesus was not primarily interested in promoting conventional economic ethics (cf. Perrin [1967] pp. 114-115), and the addition of vv. 10-13 seems a rather uncomfortable attempt to turn Jesus' obvious appeal for shrewd practice into a general renunciation of wealth. But what virtue does the lord see in the "injustice" that he praises the steward for perpetrating? This, indeed, is the crux of the parable, since only the lord's reasoning can make the steward's dealings appear as anything other than simple bribery. The second half of v. 8 provides no hint of this reasoning, consisting as it does only of further praise of "the sons of this age" for such activity, which generally is regarded as unjust (as it explicitly is in v. 8a). V. 9, however, clearly provides the justification for such "injustice": it is that "mammon of injustice" is being spent as purposefully as the steward used his master's account book. In a situation too desperate for hoarding and even for straightforward dealing, one can only spend what is not really his in the attempt to win a few friends in a world that is passing away, and our lord is such that he praises us for doing so. Because God is our master, and not an ordinary owner, what may seem to be dishonesty by ordinary standards is in his terms good stewardship, because he wants his wealth lavished on others as if there were no tomorrow. Even with v. 9, the parable cannot be reduced to a simple prose message, but at least it is made clear that the generous spending of the steward, not his selfish intention, is what the master in the parable praises.

The attitude expressed towards mammon in vv. 10-13 is consistent in the end with the sort of carelessness urged in vv. 1-9, in that non-attachment to wealth is the basic message of this appended material, while the basis of this non-attachment is made clear in the parable itself (including its closing saying). But vv. 1-9 have a different and more fundamental perspective, in that they lay a theological foundation for the attitude which puts the opportunity to benefit others

ahead of the claims of rightful ownership. Such a message
must be stated parabolically, because it reaches beyond the
limits of what can straightforwardly be said about mammon. Jesus' message is not that mammon is to be avoided,
nor that it is to be sought, saved or enjoyed. The picture he
draws is not even of disinterested altruism, but of passion-
ately using mammon to gain what mammon does not normally purchase. This activity is praised because it is what
God wishes: the logic of the parable is only apparent when
the steward's craftiness is seen, not as the mere programme
for survival he intended, but as the enactment of his master's
will. Such logic cannot be expressed in terms of the self-
interested pursuit of wealth, or of the self-interested abstention from wealth, so that ordinary, prosaic discourse about
what economic attitude is best for the individual is inappropriate. Only a picture can be offered of what otherwise
cannot be referred to, a picture of God as a gracious and
demanding master who praises skilful generosity which
looks beyond the present situation towards that which is to
develop "in eternal dwellings" (16:9 end). God, the rich
master and praising lord, appears at the beginning and end
of the parable (16:1, 8); the craftiness of the steward is only
of interest within this context, and then simply as a paradigm of the use of mammon urged in v. 9.

The picture of the steward's daring ploy, in short, remains
a picture of what God wants; we cannot turn it into a
maxim, and v. 9 certainly does not do so. The parable
represents the most desirable relationship between a person
and God that can be enjoyed, and conveys that relationship
in a picture which hints at what cannot be said openly. The
picture is largely effective because it shocks, and only appli-
cable because v. 9 provides a clue of how one might imitate
the steward's craftiness. With v. 9, the parable remains a
symbol in the proper sense: we are urged to see and act on
our relation to God in a new light, but the actual terms of
that relationship, precisely because it does not belong
entirely to the world of our ordinary experience and language, are not spelled out. Without v. 9, the parable would
be as shocking, but it would fail to convey the sense of the

lord's paradoxical behaviour, and to that extent it would leave us no wiser as to the reasons for his praise of the steward.

Reading v. 9 as the organic conclusion to the parable, in which the right disposition of "mammon of injustice" is the reason the lord praises the steward's "injustice" (v. 8), we are brought back to the observation that "mammon of injustice" refers to a form of bribery, just as "mammon of deceit" in Targum Isaiah 5:23 does. The usage of the Targum at other points (cf. 45:13; 55:1; 56:11; 57:17) shows that the connotations of "mammon" were generally, but not exclusively, negative. "Of deceit" is therefore a rather specific qualification. The rendering of the Aramaic word for "deceit" (שקר) into Greek "injustice" (ἀδικία) during the course of the transmission of the saying is not at all surprising, since both terms have a fairly general meaning, and the Greek term does sometimes render Hebrew שקר in the Septuagint. In Isaiah 33:15, moreover, Aramaic "mammon of deceit" is used to render the Hebrew phrase "profit of oppression," and "oppression" is represented by ἀδικία in the Septuagintal version of this verse. The end of the parable proper would therefore seem to be that the lord praised the steward for his clever deceit (v. 8a), followed by a general recommendation of this sort of behaviour (v. 8b) and the reasoning behind the praise: God intends mammon of deceit to be used generously in the sense described above (v. 9).

Our reading of the parable in terms of v. 9 enables us to understand why the "injustice" of the steward is praised. Any argument to the effect that the steward in the parable acted legally in changing the account book (cf. Marshall [1978] pp. 614-615, 620) must limit the reference of the steward's "injustice" in v. 8 to the period before his last deeds, which seems artificial, and even then the positive praise of the lord is anomalous. On a more straightforward reading, we suggest the deceit (שקר) of the steward is praised as a whole because he is an example of how to use the mammon of deceit (ממון דשקר). A close association between the two uses of "deceit," related as they both were to bribery in the Aramaic version of the parable, stands behind vv. 8, 9 and illuminates the meaning of the present text of Luke 16:1-9, the suitability of v. 9 to vv. 1-8 and the distinctiveness of this complex within this chapter of Luke. The pertinence of "mammon of deceit" to bribery was called to our attention by its appearance in the Isaiah Targum in order to refer to a bribe. We can therefore suggest that, through the evidence of the Targum, we have come to a clearer understanding of a parable and a saying whose very difficulty and whose coherence with other sayings (cf. Matthew 6:1-4 as well as 6:24 and Luke 16:13) suggests they are the words of Jesus. In this case, the Targum has been of use to us, not because Jesus cited it or its interpretation, even allusively, but because it employs language which corresponds to that of Jesus and, on this basis, sheds light on the precise meaning of a notoriously difficult parable and a rather enigmatic saying.

Dictional coherences between the Isaiah Targum and sayings of Jesus which do not refer to Isaiah are, however, not only of the generally linguistic type investigated above. In Matthew 7:2 and Mark 4:24, Jesus warns his hearers, "in the measure you measure it will be measured to you." In Matthew, this warning is given point with the parable of the splinter in one's brother's eye (vv. 3-5), while in Mark it is part of a series of sayings which calls for the attentive hearing and understanding of parables (vv. 22-25, cf. v. 13). The application of the saying therefore differs according to context, yet in both cases it is used without explanation, as if it would be readily taken in. As a matter of fact, the statement that a man is measured by his own standard frequently occurs in Talmud, and under the names of various rabbis, for example Ḥiyya bar Abba (citing Joḥanan, Shabbath 105b), Meir (Sanhedrin 100a) and Rabbi (Sotah 8b). The obvious inference from the rabbinic evidence is that the saying is a maxim, and this opens the possibility that it was also proverbial in the time of Jesus (cf. Strack — Billerbeck [1926] pp. 444-445; McNamara [1966] pp. 138f.; Rüger [1969] pp. 174-182).

Against this background, a passage in the Isaiah Targum

is particularly interesting. At 27:8, the Hebrew text of Isaiah is difficult of interpretation (cf. Gray [1912] pp. 457-458; Young II [1969] pp. 243-245), but the Targum presents quite a free paraphrase at this point in order to convey a clear meaning:

> In the measure you were measuring with they will measure you...

Apparently, the first word in the Hebrew text, which is similar to the term for a third of an ephah, was taken to imply measurement, and the proverbial saying was therefore incorporated at this point. (A similar phenomenon, but without the express citation of the maxim, is evident in some manuscripts of the Septuagint.) The use of the maxim in the Targum strengthens the case for the argument that it was current in the time and language circle of Jesus, but the particular form of the maxim in the Targum deserves special attention as compared to its form in the New Testament. The rabbinic proverb appears in the third person, but the second person is used in the Targum, just as in Jesus' saying. To this extent, the Targumic reading brings us closest to the saying of Jesus substantively as well as chronologically.

Nonetheless, there are dissimilarities between the Targumic and dominical versions of the proverb. The Targumic interpreter speaks in the singular of the second person, while Jesus uses the plural, and "you were measuring," not "you measure" appears in the text of the former. The plural usage by Jesus should not be pressed too hard as conveying the essential meaning of the saying, however, since in both Matthew (7:3) and Mark (4:25) the proverb is immediately followed by material in which a singular form is used. An aphoristic warning can be spoken in either the singular or the plural, and in fact one can see a mixture of the two in the Gospel tradition itself, so that this distinction between the Targumic and New Testament versions of the proverb should not be seen as significant. Similarly, the fact that the word "with" appears in the Targum after "you were measuring," but not in the corresponding position in Matthew or

Mark, reflects only an idiomatic peculiarity of Aramaic as compared to Greek. The difference in tenses between the two versions is more significant, and the present tense is perhaps more suitable to a proverb than the past tense. The latter may be used in the Targum, not because it was proverbial, but because this passage from Isaiah implicitly deals with past transgression. It seems that the Aramaic proverb which Jesus also cites has been altered somewhat in the Targum to take account of the biblical passage it renders. Our suspicion that this is the case is confirmed when we observe that the opening word for "measure" in the Targum corresponds to the first letters of the Hebrew text, with the result that it differs more from the verb "measure" than was necessary, and more than we might expect from a proverb in Aramaic, in that the repetition of similar sounds is a characteristic feature of Aramaic maxims. Even the altered wording of the Targum, however, is a close parallel to the maxim as used by Jesus, and it confirms that he is citing a proverb at this point. The propriety of this saying within Jesus' preaching is rightly emphasized by Rudolf Pesch (1976, p. 253), who cites Matthew 5:25f.; 7:1; 25:14-30, 31-46; Luke 19:11-27 by way of comparison to demonstrate that this thought was basic to his teaching. In his presentation of this motif, Jesus seems to have been developing the folk wisdom of his day, not offering a completely new thought. The probability is therefore that the Gospels rightly give the impression that Jesus used the maxim on different occasions.

The instances of New Testament coherence with the Isaiah Targum so far discussed have all involved explicitly dominical sayings. One further case should also be mentioned in this section, although the New Testament passage in question is not attributed to Jesus. In the baptismal narratives of Matthew, Mark and Luke, Jesus is the reference of a heavenly voice:

> "This is my son, the beloved, in whom I am well pleased"
> (Matthew 3:17);

> "You are my son, the beloved; in you I am well pleased"
> (Mark 1:11);

"You are my son, the beloved; in you I am well pleased" (Luke 3:22).

T. W. Manson argued that these words, along with the account of the baptism as a whole, must have derived from Jesus himself on the grounds that in Mark Jesus alone is portrayed as having the vision and hearing the voice (1955, p. 103).

The evidence is, however, a bit more complex than this argument would suggest. Luke, it is true, only refers to the descent of the spirit and the voice after he mentions Jesus was baptized and was praying (3:21). But this may only manifest Luke's tendency to play down John's place in the scene. He tells of the Baptist's arrest before he relates the baptism (3:19, 20), and says Jesus' baptism occurred "when all the people were baptized." Faced with Luke's text alone, we might not even conclude that John personally baptized Jesus, and the reference to Jesus' prayer as the immediate context of the descent of the spirit and the explanatory voice underlines the distinction between what happened to Jesus and the usual experience of baptism within the movement founded by John. Such a distinction is fully consistent with the insistence in Acts that the spirit is associated with baptism into Jesus' name, not with John's baptism in itself (cf. Acts 19:1-7), and also with Luke's tendency in the opening material in the Gospel to present John and Jesus material contrapuntally in discrete blocks. In none of this is there any apparent desire on Luke's part to emphasize that only Jesus saw the vision and heard the voice, both of which are (as in Matthew) described in objective terms. Moreover, both Matthew (3:16) and Mark (1:10) place the vision immediately after the (public) baptism, and refer to the voice objectively. Manson would therefore seem to have placed too much stress on the fact Mark says Jesus saw the heavens open and the spirit descend (v. 10), and it is far from certain, as he assumed, that Mark also set the voice apart as a private event (v. 11).

The rabbinic conception of the *bath qol* ("daughter," or echo, "of a voice") has obvious similarities to the baptismal voice, and the former is viewed as an objective phenomenon in Rabbinica, where the echo was understood as a sound which proceeded from a heavenly voice, and so as the contemporary counterpart of God's address to his people through the prophets (cf. Strack — Billerbeck [1926] pp. 125-134). Nonetheless, the *bath qol* in Rabbinica, although objective, is not consistently portrayed as public; a particular rabbi often attests the message, and in the New Testament we also find such a voice in a subjective (indeed, in a visionary) context (cf. Acts 10:9-16). The example of Peter's experience in Acts is particularly striking in respect of the baptism of Jesus because — as in the Gospel according to Luke — private prayer is given as the occasion of the vision and the voice. The voice in Acts, with which Peter enters into dialogue, contradicts the current view of what constitutes uncleanness, and in so doing alludes to and corrects Ezekiel 4:9-17. The voice of the baptismal accounts is not so dramatically portrayed, nor does it stand in such obvious tension to a particular Old Testament passage. But — as we will see below — the baptismal voice must also be said at least to use biblical language creatively, and in this degree the passage from Acts is also illuminating. Finally, as in the Acts account of Peter's experience during prayer, the baptismal account presents the divine testimony through a *bath qol* which only the principal of the passage (Peter or Jesus) is named as hearing. Whether others could or did hear anything is beside the point: the attestation of the voice is given as through the principal, not anyone else. In the case of Peter in Acts, the principal formally recounts his experience in order to justify his new attitude to Gentiles (cf. Acts 11:4-10). Jesus, of course, is not portrayed as ever speaking directly of his baptism, and yet the baptismal voice is the only form of directly divine warrant ever given for Jesus' admission that he was God's son (cf. Matthew 26:63-64; Mark 14:61-62; Luke 22:70). In this indirect sense, the baptismal voice might be considered within a treatment of Jesus' sayings: the words are not attributed to him, but they are presented as being crucial to his understanding of his own mission and identity.

The terms used by the voice sound biblical, but there seems to be no question of an actual citation of a biblical passage. As parallel to the use of the term "beloved," Robert Gundry (1967, p. 30) cites the Aramaic Targum to Psalm 2:7, and in fact this passage is frequently cited (not only in its Aramaic form) as providing at least part of the background of the biblical voice (cf. Anderson [1976] pp. 79-80; Marshall [1978] p. 155). But the wording of the Psalm at this point ("You are my son, this day have I begotten you") is quite different from the baptismal acclamation, even if one adds the word "dear" or "beloved" (חביב), as in the (undoubtedly late) Psalms Targum. Moreover, the Matthean voice, in the third person rather than in the second is — practically speaking — unrecognizable as even an allusion to the Psalm. In any case, the only reason the question of a parallel between the voice and Psalm has been discussed is probably that an actual citation of Psalm 2:7 is a variant reading in the Gospel according to Luke (notably, in the Codex Bezae). But this variant itself appears to be an attempt to make the voice into a quotation from the Bible, which — in most of the best New Testament manuscripts —it does not seem to be.

The Matthean voice is much closer to Isaiah 42:1, the other biblical passage commonly cited as the reference at issue (cf. Hill [1972] p. 97; Anderson [1976] p. 79; Marshall [1978] p. 155). With the change of person already noted, this reference seems more possible, especially when one bears in mind that, in 12:18, Matthew actually cites this passage in Isaiah by name (cf. v. 17), using the terms "beloved" and "to be well pleased." (In so doing, he offers a version of the Isaian text which differs markedly from the Septuagint, although also from the Targum.) But even the wording of Matthew 12:18 is quite different from Matthew 3:17 (cf. Hooker [1959] pp. 70f.), and even more so from the Markan and Lukan versions of the voice's statement. In the second person, as in Mark and Luke, the voice is even further removed from Isaiah 42:1 than in Matthew, and Matthew himself — in his explicit citation of Isaiah 42:1 with different words — seems to presuppose the voice is not a citation. The reason for Matthew's change of persons (in comparison with Mark and Luke) seems to be to bring the baptismal *bath qol* into line with the *bath qol* at the transfiguration (17:5, cf. "this" and "in whom I am well pleased"; Chilton [1980³]), not to accommodate the baptismal voice to any particular Old Testament passage. The idea that the voice is an actual citation appears more and more dubious (cf. Suhl [1965] p. 103).

The argument that Isaiah 42:1 is in the background of the narrative of Jesus' baptism is much easier to sustain on the ground that the spirit is mentioned in the passage (so Marshall [1978] p. 156). Nonetheless, the voice does not mention the spirit, so that this argument cannot be pressed to the point of saying that Isaiah 42:1 is quoted or alluded to by the voice. One of the major difficulties with such an assertion is that the "I am well pleased" of the voice does not correspond to the phrasing of the versions of Isaiah at this point, "my soul is well pleased" (Hebrew), "my soul accepts" (Greek), "my word is well pleased" (Aramaic). On the other hand, the phrase "I am well pleased" turns up fairly frequently in the Targum when the verb "to choose" (בחר or ἐκλέγομαι) is employed in the Hebrew and Greek versions:

Isaiah 41:8-9
Targum — "You, Israel my servant, Jacob that (or: in whom [ד]) I am well pleased with you... I said to you, you are my servant, I am well pleased with you...';
Hebrew — "You, Israel my servant, Jacob that (or: in whom [אשׁר]) I chose you... I said to you, you are my servant, I chose you...";
Greek — "And you Israel, my servant Jacob, whom I chose... I said to you, you are my servant, I chose you...";

Isaiah 43:10
Targum — "...my servant the messiah that (or: in whom [ד]) I am well pleased with him...";
Hebrew — "...and my servant that (or: whom [אשׁר]) I chose...";
Greek — "...and my servant whom I chose...."

In addition to the use of the precise phrase, "I am well pleased" (for which see also 43:20 and 44:1-2), it is perhaps also significant that 41:8, 9 present the usage in a solemn address, and that 43:10 identifies the servant as the messiah. That is, we have in the Targum alone an idiom which corresponds to the expression of the baptismal voice, and which has a range of associations — the direct address of 41:8, 9, the references to the spirit in 42:1 and the messiah in 43:10 — which suits the usage of this expression by the voice in the narrative of Jesus' baptism.

At this point, we might reasonably assert that the baptismal voice does not cite words from a particular scriptural passage, but uses language associated with a figure called "the servant." The term "servant" (Aramaic עבדא or טליא) was evidently taken up in the Gospel tradition in its relational sense to form part of the identification of Jesus as God's "son" which was also a term of relation in the most primitive usage (cf. Jeremias [1954] p. 699; Hengel [1976] pp. 21f.). We can see a similar development in usage when we compare the Synoptic account of the healing of the centurion's servant (or child: παῖς) with the Johannine account of the healing of the royal official's son (Matthew 8:5-13; Luke 7:1-10; John 4:46-54). Of course, each use of the term "son" in the Greek New Testament by no means necessarily reflects a use of "servant" in Aramaic Gospel tradition; the point is simply that "son" and "servant," when their emphasis is on a close relationship between God and a particular person, should be seen as bearing a somewhat similar theological meaning, so that the use of the term "son" in the words of the baptismal voice need not be taken to refer to a figure who is qualitatively different from the servant in the Targumic "I am well pleased" passages. The term "beloved," corresponding best to יחיד (not חביב) in Hebrew and Aramaic, is also a relational term, and implies that an in some sense unique relationship subsists between a person and God (cf. F. Lentzen-Deis [1970] pp. 228-243). With "son," then, the term "beloved" should be regarded as generally biblical, and as consistent with the apparently Targumic idiom used by the voice, without proving that a figure such as the servant in Isaiah is in mind. The question whether Jesus used the imagery of the Targumic servant in order to convey the sense of his own ministry is to be treated separately (cf. Appendix I); although — as we will see — this possibility cannot be excluded, and, indeed, the prophetic vocation of the servant in the Targum corresponds in large measure to Jesus' own view of his relation to God, there is no question of his citing a Targumic servant passage as if it specified his own purpose and fate exactly. In the present case also, the voice which speaks of Jesus as "son" does so in the language of intimate relation, such as is applied to the servant in the Targum. No complete identification between Jesus and the servant is therefore posited, but — at the very moment in which, according to the Synoptic tradition, Jesus' public ministry began — Targumic servant language is given as the starting point for understanding Jesus in his relation to God.

A2 FINDINGS

In this section, we have uncovered a small but surprisingly diverse group of passages which evidence coherence between the Targum and Jesus' sayings. Consideration of the first (Luke 16:9) suggests that the theological language used by Jesus is reflected in the Targum, while the second (Matthew 7:2; Mark 4:24) evidences Jesus' express quotation of a popular proverb which is best preserved (outside the New Testament) in the Targum. In both of these cases, the service performed by the Targum in providing a parallel to Jesus' usage is that the actual meaning of his words becomes clearer to us. "Mammon of deceit" seems to have to do with the sort of bribery the parable of the unjust steward commends, and the saying in which it appears proves to be an intrinsic part of the preceding parable. The "measure" saying is shown to invoke a proverb from the store of the folk wisdom of Jesus' time in order to illuminate the relations between people and God. The third case, that of the baptismal voice (Matthew 3:17; Mark 1:11; Luke 3:22), is perhaps an especially interesting instance of coher-

ence with the Targum. Since the support for the argument
that the voice represents an actual citation from scripture
has been reviewed and found wanting, we have been able to
offer a new understanding of the background of the words
used. The baptismal election of Jesus has proved not to
consist of his complete identification with an Old Testament
figure (such as "the servant," much less "the suffering servant"), but to convey his divine authorization in biblical or
Targumic terms; it is a selection of a person — the commendation of a son — without predetermining his precise role.

Obviously, however, the Targumic background of the
words used by the baptismal voice raises questions which
the "mammon" and "measure" sayings do not. The latter
two are widely regarded as being authentically dominical,
that is, as historical in the full sense of being significant,
meaningful and authentic. Because the explanation of
Jesus' baptism as a function of his relationship with God is
attributed to a divine voice, we may well find that our
attitude towards these words differs radically from our
attitude towards the others. We might feel ourselves more in
the sort of situation we are in when we read of exorcisms
than we are in when we read parables, because the many
bath qol references in Rabbinica do not alleviate the difficulties we face when narratives refer to such phenomena.
The significance and meaning of Jesus' baptism are apparent; as has been mentioned, the designation of Jesus as son
by a specifically divine voice is the only full substantiation
provided in the Gospels for the admission Jesus makes that
he is God's son. The voice at the transfiguration (Matthew
17:5; Mark 9:7; Luke 9:35) would seem to refer back to the
baptismal voice (cf. Chilton [1980[3]]). The demonic identification of Jesus as God's son (Matthew 8:29; Mark 3:11; 5:7;
Luke 4:41; 8:28) is obviously a subsidiary matter, as is the
clearly secondary use of the identification in Luke 1:32, 35;
Matthew 14:33. The usages at Matthew 4:3, 6; Luke 4:3, 9
and Matthew 27:40, 43, 54; Mark 15:39 are all presented on
the understanding that Jesus' identity as God's son is
already taken as read. In this sense, the voice appears to
express not only an essential aspect of the message of the

Gospels, but also one of Jesus' determinative convictions. Whether such a voice actually spoke, however, and whether it can have spoken, is not for the historian to say. That a *bath qol* would not be an unexpected feature in the ministry of a popular and successful rabbi/healer in this period is obvious from the Jewish sources, and the voice seems to be an inextricable part of Jesus' awareness — right or wrong —of who he was in relation to God. That Jesus believed he heard such a voice is as close as one could come to asserting its historical authenticity in critical terms, and at the same time one must make this sort of assertion in order to explain Jesus' admission to the Temple authorities (cf. also Matthew 11:27; Luke 10:22). The Targumic colouring of the message of the voice substantiates this finding, because it places the *bath qol* in the same tradition critical category as the authentically dominical sayings already treated. The tenor of the voice, as it were, is that of Jesus, in that the usage of idioms also evidenced in the Targum is characteristically dominical. Not only the meaning, then, but also the authenticity of the voice as a phenomenon which Jesus took seriously have been illuminated by a consideration of the Isaiah Targum.

B2 INSTANCES OF THEMATIC COHERENCE WITH THE TARGUM IN OTHER SAYINGS OF JESUS

One of the characteristic themes of the Tannaitic framework of the Isaiah Targum is that of the persistent refusal of God's people to attend to the announcement of the prophets and repent. It is a remarkable instance of the thematic coherence between the Targum and Jesus' preaching that he voiced the same complaint. For Jesus, the refusal to hear the prophets is both consistent and systematic (Matthew 5:12; Luke 6:23); the Isaian interpreter also lamented that "with strange speech and mocking tongue these people were ridiculing the prophets who prophesied to them" (28:11). A similar point of view lies behind several dominical sayings (notably Matthew 13:57; Mark 6:4; Luke 4:24; John 4:44), and in the Targum the refusal to repent is seen as so chronic that God responds by stilling prophecy (29:10, for an explanation of the theme in the Targum, cf. Chilton [1982] pp. 52-56). The refusal to hear the prophets was so extreme, as Jesus understood it, that it even led to murder (cf. Matthew 23:29-32, 34-37; Luke 11:47-51; 13:33-34). Such a dramatic description of violence directed specifically against the prophets is not to be found in the Targum, but it is notable that Jesus' sayings are pointed against Jerusalem in particular (Matthew 23:37; Luke 13:34), and then with a cultic reference (Matthew 23:35; Luke 11:51), just as the programmatic Targumic reference (28:11) to the failure to hear the prophets occurs in a chapter which repeatedly refers to the inadequate conduct of the Temple cult in Jerusalem proper (cf. also 29:1). The theme of the rejection of the prophets by their own people, and that of the prophetic opposition to contemporary worship is therefore a common element between Jesus and the Targum, while the vivid depiction of their persecution in Jesus' preaching is not paralleled in the Targum.

The last-mentioned element of Jesus' preaching appears to have been a common feature of the first-century Jewish understanding of the fate of the prophets (cf. O. H. Steck [1967]). Particularly, the document curiously named "The Lives of the Prophets" (Torrey [1946]) — which vividly depicts the apocryphal martyrdoms of the prophets — reflects legendary developments in traditions about the prophets which apparently influenced Jesus. Although — as Pierre Grelot (1972) has shown — there was an attempt to incorporate this motif in an Aramaic version of Isaiah, it is only reflected in the isolated readings of fragmentary textual witnesses. The Targum which has come down to us apparently never included such references, which seem to come from a different tradition of interpretation. (Stylistically, the readings, especially at 66:1, are much more discursive than one normally finds in this Targum, which confirms our suspicion as to the oddity of the subject matter.) In the end, therefore, the Targumic coherence with Jesus' preaching is quite definitely imperfect in this instance, although the evidence to some extent encourages the view that certain variant readings in the full tradition of Targumic readings might inform us of theological currents and fashions in the time of Jesus.

The focus on Israel in the theology of the Isaian framework interpreters leads to the expression of an exclusivist theology of revelation:

> You have heard; has what is revealed to you been revealed to any other people? (48:6).

As in the case of the motif in respect of the prophets discussed above, however, the present theme is the common property of early Judaism and rabbinic Judaism. Israel is consistently reminded of the special favour and revelation (above all, the revelation of the law) which God has given to him (cf. 28:9, Avoth 3:15 and, for further citations and discussion, Chilton [1982] pp. 13-18, 33-37). A theme of exclusivity is also prominent among the sayings of Jesus, above all in the famous declaration:

> Amen I say to you that many prophets and just men wished to see what you see and did not see, and to hear what you hear and did not hear (Matthew 13:17; cf. Luke 10:24).

The language of limitation and exclusion is here being used within Israel, not in order to speak of Israel as distinct from the nations. Moreover, the reference to the prophets as those who did not attain to what the disciples experience is an extraordinarily bold innovation, especially given the veneration for the prophets among Jesus' contemporaries (which is discussed in the preceding paragraph). The authenticity of the saying is not a matter of dispute, and is confirmed by its originality and by its obviously foundational importance for the development of New Testament theology (cf. 1 Peter 1:10-12; Hebrews 11:39-40). The Targumic theme of the exclusive revelation to Israel is, as in the previous case, only partially similar to a theme in Jesus' preaching, and here the departure of Jesus from the early Judaism of his day (which the Targum does seem to reflect) is in any case more determinative of the significance of the saying than any such partial coherence with the Targum.

B2 FINDINGS

This section is emphatically the least significant in the treatment of four categories of coherence offered here, and the two cases discussed do not evidence any specific contact between Jesus and the Isaiah Targum, or even between Jesus and the tradition behind the Targum. To a limited extent, the early Judaism of which Jesus was a product is reflected in the Targum, and both 28:11 and 48:6 in the Aramaic version of Isaiah perhaps instance the usefulness of the Targum for understanding the background against which Jesus spoke. In each instance, however, the insight offered by the Targumic reading merely confirms what we could infer from other sources, anyway; whatever the value of the Targum in particular cases, it should not be treated as the sole, or even as a uniquely important, witness to early Judaism. This warning is particularly pertinent to the prophetic motif in the Targum, which does not reflect an early Jewish emphasis on the violent death of the prophets which influenced Jesus. Even the difference in focus between the exclusivity theme of Jesus and that expressed in the Targum is perhaps not merely the result of innovation on Jesus' part. Other Jews in his period used exclusivist language of groups or movements within Israel — most obviously, John the Baptist (cf. Matthew 3:7-10; Luke 3:7-9) and the Qumran community (cf. the programmatic differentiation between "the sons of light" and "the sons of darkness" in the *War Scroll*) — so that one would best refrain even in this case from making global generalizations to the effect that Jesus transformed the categories of Judaism. We have already observed that the period of provenience of the earlier Targumic framework saw a threat to Israel's national identity of such a magnitude that the Aramaic interpreters responded by expressing their faith and hope in profoundly nationalistic terms. This may well have influenced the use of the language of exclusivity in the Targum, so that the distinction between Jesus' usage and that of the interpreters might just be a function of the development of national consciousness in early Judaism after the ministry of Jesus.

3. Conclusions

The kingdom theology of the Isaiah Targum, as compared with that of Jesus' preaching, was the starting point of our analysis. Although the substantive agreement that the kingdom refers to God's personal and dynamic intervention on behalf of his people is important, the coherence between Jesus and the Targum is far from perfect: the Targum's theology of messianic vindication put the kingdom in a more nationalistic perspective, while Jesus' attitude to those on the fringes of or outside Judaism was notoriously liberal. To some extent this distinction is the result of developments in Targumic tradition after the time of Jesus; earlier Targumic interpretations of the kingdom are less exclusivist. The relationship between Jesus and the Targum is therefore a matter for critical reflection. The question for us was not first of all whether Jesus used the Isaiah Targum, but whether interpretative traditions later incorporated in the Targum had a formative influence on the wording of some sayings attributed to Jesus. Since this influence was most likely exerted at an early stage in the formation of the sayings as we know them, coherence with Targumic diction was seen to be significant in deciding whether a saying reflected Jesus' position more than interpretative adaptations of his words.

The first category of coherence (A1) contains references to Isaiah in Jesus' sayings which evince a substantive verbal similarity with the Targum. The case of Mark 4:11, 12 was treated, and while the experience of the pre-Markan church was held to be reflected in v. 11, v. 12 was seen to manifest Jesus' characterization of his hearers in terms borrowed from the Targum (6:9, 10). Jesus also seems in Matthew 26:52 to have referred to a Targumic proverb (50:11) in a paraphrastic and abbreviated manner. The association in Mark 9:47, 48 of "Gehenna" with a citation of Isaiah 66:24 is best explained with recourse to the Targum, and the use of the citation as a refrain (in vv. 44, 46) appeared to evidence the awareness on the part of early tradents of Jesus' message that the Targumic interpretation of his day was significant to the understanding of his teaching. In each case, the correspondence with the Targum shed light on the questions of the development, authenticity and meaning of the saying.

We acknowledged from the outset that our next category of thematic coherence between the Targum and dominical references to Isaiah (B1), could not be held to contain evidence as probative of the connection between the Targum and Jesus' sayings as that cited under the previous category. Since thematic similarity is here analyzed, the treatment is necessarily less empirical as compared to a consideration of dictional similarity. Nonetheless, we found that the parable of the vineyard (Matthew 21:33-46; Mark 12:1-12; Luke 20:9-19), in its specific application to Israel's leaders especially, is reminiscent of the Targumic interpretation of Isaiah 5:1-7. To this extent, the parable was probably told by Jesus himself, although it was embellished by his followers so as to take account of his own death. The Targumic interpretation also underwent substantial development after the time of Jesus, and refers to the catastrophic events which took place around 70 A.D.

Certain sayings of Jesus, although they are not explicit quotations of Isaiah, employ diction found in the Isaiah Targum (category A2). The phrase "mammon of injustice" in Luke 16:9 was related to "mammon of deceit" in Targum Isaiah 5:23 (cf. 33:15), and we suggested on this basis that the Lukan expression refers to the bribery of the steward, which is commended in the parable as a paradigm for the economics of discipleship. More straightforwardly, the Targumic proverb, "In the measure you were measuring they will measure you" (27:8), was found to stand back of Matthew 7:2 and Mark 4:24, so that Jesus appears here to have adapted a folk saying of his day. The use of the phrase "I am well pleased" in the Targum (cf. 41:8-9; 42:1; 43:10) provides a range of associations which makes its appearance in the words of the baptismal *bath qol* (Matthew 3:17; Mark 1:11; Luke 3:22) understandable. The meaning of the saying at Luke 16:9, and the parable in which it appears, was illuminated by the Targumic precedent, and the proverbial nature of Matthew 7:2; Mark 4:24 was established. Moreover, the words of the baptismal voice were found to be consistent— tradition critically—with Jesus' own sayings.

Jesus complained that the announcement of the prophets was consistently rejected, and a similar complaint is found in the Targum: this similarity occasioned the category of thematic coherence between the Targum and dominical sayings in which Isaiah is not cited (B2). None of the evidence cited under this category, however, enabled us to claim any special connection between Jesus and the Targum or its tradition, in that the motif in question is characteristic of early Judaism generally. Moreover, while the Targum speaks of the exclusivity of Israel as God's chosen people, Jesus refers to the exclusivity of some within Israel, of their special favour even as compared to the prophets. In this case, the dissimilarity between Jesus' sayings and the Targum is more significant than any coherence, although it must be remembered that the Targum, framed largely during the experience of war against Rome, was probably rather more nationalistic than some at least of its constituent traditions.

We have repeatedly cautioned that Jesus did not depend on the Targum as we know it, but he does seem to have been influenced and informed by traditions which the Targum preserves better than anything else. The present (deliberately succinct) summary points out the range of evidence on which this conclusion is based, and — together with the exegetical treatment which precedes — establishes that our suggestion is a reasonable inference from the data to hand. Moreover, our consideration of the relationship between Jesus and the Targum has enabled us to contribute answers to certain key questions in respect of the New Testament passages adduced: their meaning (Mark 4:12; Luke 16:9; Matthew 21:33-46; Mark 12:1-12; Luke 20:9-19), their genre (Matthew 26:52; Matthew 7:2; Mark 4:24), their authenticity (Mark 9:48; Matthew 3:17; Mark 1:11; Luke 3:22). The fact that certain sayings can be better understood within a treatment of our suggestion itself supports the thesis, and also indicates that our argument concerns, not only the origin of Jesus' message, but also its proper interpretation. His relationship with the Targum, and perhaps with other Targums, is of significance for students of Jesus' ministry as a whole. The question of the origin of Jesus' sayings naturally involves the issue of authenticity, and the similarity of a saying to Targumic material has provided a tradition critical parameter in evaluating the extent to which Jesus actually said what is attributed to him and the extent to which his message has been interpreted during the course of its transmission. Particularly, we would recall our distinctions between verse 11 and verse 12 of Mark 4, between v. 48 and vv. 44, 46 of Mark 9, and between strata in the formation of the present parable of the vineyard by way of insisting that evidence of coherence between a saying and the Targum has here occasioned critical consideration, and has not been taken as an unequivocal seal of authenticity. Precisely for this reason, our handling of the baptismal voice tradition has been circumspect and of a preliminary nature.

To a slight degree, the influence of traditions preserved in the Isaiah Targum seems to have been felt during the period of the transmission of Jesus' sayings. Although Jesus' own citation of such tradition is the best explanation for Mark 4:12, v. 11 shows that the Targumic form of citation occasioned an interpretation in the life of the early Church designed to claim an exclusive understanding of Jesus' message among the Twelve and their associates. Then, too, the repeated citation, in respect of Gehenna, of Isaiah 66:24 in some manuscripts at Mark 9:44, 46 would indicate the awareness of early tradents of Jesus' words that he referred to Targumic traditions, and would further suggest that this tradition was sufficiently well known in the early Church to justify its usage as a refrain. In the case of the parable of the vineyard, however, the secondary elements —which seem evident — do not appear to have been occasioned by Targumic tradition or by an acknowledgement of Jesus' recourse to such tradition. The evidence for a tendency to accommodate Jesus' sayings to Targumic tradition is therefore thin; indeed, one can really only say on the basis of the evidence we have considered that Targumic associations already present in his sayings occasionally resulted in further developments in these associations by the tradents of the Jesus tradition. For this reason, one might argue that the baptismal voice—which is not, after all, actually ascribed to Jesus—might owe its Targumic coloration to such primitive tradents. On the other hand, this coloration is rather more characteristic of Jesus' usage than of his disciples', so that it is perhaps more plausible to argue that the account of Jesus' baptism was at least partially developed during Jesus' life and under his influence. This is obviously a matter for further discussion, and we have found again and again that historical questions cannot be bypassed by determining the tradition critical pedigree of a saying; tradition critical data merely provide some of the evidence on which a sound historical judgment may be based.

By far, however, the most striking discovery of our study has been that Jesus himself referred to the tradition of the Isaiah Targum in the course of articulating his message. This fact alone speaks volumes in respect of Jesus' attitude to the early Judaism of his day; he not only accepted the written Bible, as is sometimes claimed, but also found the tradition of his time as developed by his folk and rabbinic colleagues to be positively valuable and useful. At times, he used material we know from the Isaiah Targum as one might employ a proverb (cf. Matthew 26:52; Matthew 7:2; Mark 4:24), and this attests the degree to which he presupposed his hearers' familiarity with this tradition. If we had only evidence of this type, one might reasonably observe that the Targum conceivably just happens best to preserve material which in the time of Jesus had nothing to do with the book of Isaiah. This possiblity, which cannot be excluded altogether, appears less likely in view of other evidence to hand. For, when in the cases of the parable of the vineyard and Mark 9:48, Jesus seems explicitly to refer to Isaiah, his reference best accords with the Targumic contexts of the passages concerned, and his citation of Isaiah at Mark 4:12 most closely approximates the text of the Targum as we can read it today. In the case of the parable of the vineyard (Matthew 21:33-46; Mark 12:1-12; Luke 20:9-19), moreover, Jesus presupposes a degree of precise familiarity with the Targum on the part of his opponents, who apparently did in the event understand that he applied the vineyard imagery of Isaiah 5 to the Temple, as in the Targum. Lastly, Luke 16:9 evidences an important dictional coherence between Jesus and the Targum.

Our general conclusion in respect of the relationship between Jesus and the Targum is based upon the evidence reviewed, but a pattern emerges from this evidence which is also worth considering in its own right. Repeatedly, Jesus seems to have used Targumic material in order to characterize people and situations. This is obviously the case in Mark 4:12, where Jesus invokes Isaiah 6:9, 10 to express frustration at his hearers' sluggish response and to demand something better. But the agreement here with the Targumic text is far from exact, and this reminds us that Jesus refers to Targumic tradition, probably in oral form, in order to articulate and enliven his message, not in order to comment expressly on that tradition. The situation is similar in respect of Matthew 26:52, where Targum Isaiah 50:11 is alluded to in a radically abbreviated way for the purpose of reminding the disciples of the attitude required by their own synagogue tradition. Even Mark 9:48 — which is a relatively straightforward quotation — finds its connection to Targum Isaiah 66:24 only implicitly, in that it deals with "Gehenna" (cf. v. 47). In all of these instances, the pattern seems reasonably clear; Jesus is no exegete, consciously attempting to interpret the Targum or its tradition, but plays on the familiarity of his semi-literate hearers with such traditions in order to evoke a vivid picture of their situation vis-à-vis God in powerful, quasi-biblical, terms. His approach is not scholarly, but homiletic; his concern is with the practical attitude of his hearers, not with a written text or a remembered tradition for its own sake.

The case of the parable of the vineyard is somewhat different. In this instance, because he is dealing with educated opponents, Jesus can play on his hearers' knowledge of Targumic interpretation in a rather subtle way, referring only to the vineyard of Isaiah five, and leaving it to his audience to make the connection — via the Targum — of their own administration of the Temple. This is the only passage in which Jesus' reference to the Targumic tradition seems to have been self-conscious; the other instances can easily be ascribed to a basically reflexive recourse to the religious vocabulary of his time. The usage in Luke 16·9, which — as we saw — appears to reflect a Targumic idiom without having the Targum in view, better represents Jesus' natural and unself-conscious tendency to refer to Targumic interpretation of Isaiah.

Against the background of a pattern established by the key connections between Jesus and the Targum discussed in part two as a whole, certain other possible connections might be cited. These have been considered in the course of researching and writing the present volume, but they appear to be neither as substantial as those discussed above, nor as probative of Jesus' use of Targumic interpretation. For these reasons, they will only be mentioned briefly here, in the hope they might be an incentive to further study.

In his sermon on the mount (Matthew 5:6), Matthew has Jesus refer to "those who hunger and thirst for righteousness," while Luke refers to people "who hunger" (6:21). Rather similarly, the Targum provides an explanation of the hunger and thirst mentioned in Isaiah 32:6; reference is made to "the righteous who desire teaching even as a hungry man bread, and words of the law, which they (desire) as a thirsty man water." No doubt, "righteousness" represents a typically Matthean emphasis in the presentation of Jesus' sayings; the term does not occur at all in Mark and appears only once in Luke, while Matthew uses it seven times. As these occurrences are always in sayings of Jesus, the term should be regarded as a hallmark of the Jesus tradition as presented by Matthew, not simply as a redactional trait. The wording of the explanation in Matthew 5:6 is therefore typically Matthean, but on the other hand cannot be regarded as necessarily secondary (cf. McNeile [1915] p. 51). The explanation in the Targum of the metaphor of hunger and thirst is clearly different from that in Matthew, and corresponds to the focus on the law in the framework, but the tendency to spell out the images in ethical terms can be counted as a similarity between Jesus' saying and the Targumic interpretation.

With considerable variation in wording, the phrase "this adulterous and sinful generation" recurs in Jesus' preaching (cf. Mark 8:38 with 9:19 and Matthew 12:39, 45; 16:4; 17:17; Luke 9:41), and serves to give his message a great deal of force. As W. L. Lane remarks (1974, p. 310), the device is generally reminiscent of the preaching of the prophets against their contemporaries. The Targum to Isaiah provides a more exact analogy, although — as in the case of Matthew 5:6 — one could not argue on this basis that there is an actual connection between Jesus and the Targum. At Isaiah 57:3, where in the Masoretic text an address which is somewhat similar to Jesus' usage already appears (cf. the Septuagint), we find a more exact, albeit rather wordy parallel in the Targum:

MT And you, come near, here, sons of a sorceress, adulterous seed, and she is faithless;

Tg And you, come near, here, people of a generation whose deeds are evil, whose plant is from a holy plant, and they are adulterous and faithless;

LX But you, come here, lawless sons, seed of adulterers and a harlot.

Adultery and faithlessness are in the Targum, as in the dominical usage, directly predicated of those addressed, and the term "generation" is also used. This is not the case in the Septuagint, and while the words "adulterers" and "harlot" are very distantly similar to what we have at Matthew 12:39; 16:4, the wording is in fact not the same and the syntax quite different. Jesus' characterization of his contemporaries could, in turn, only be said to be broadly similar to what we find in the Targum, but the affinity between the two, even if largely conceptual, is rather striking.

The additional two cases here discussed appear to belong to the same pattern which we saw emerge when we compared Jesus' sayings to their (more firmly established) Targumic antecedents; Jesus' usage seems to have been more succinct than that which appears in the Targumic interpretation, and quite innovative when judged against the standard of the Targum. If one were thoroughly convinced that Jesus was familiar directly with the tradition of the Isaiah Targum which we have access to in written form, one would be able to trace its influence on other sayings (cf. Appendix II). That, however, is for further research to establish; the present inquiry has simply permitted us to maintain that Jesus knew an exegetical tradition associated with the book of Isaiah which is substantially preserved in the Isaiah Targum, and that he took his hearers' familiarity with that tradition for granted. This finding has given us an insight into Jesus' use of this exegetical tradition, an insight which we hope to pursue further in the next part of our study.

Our findings in respect of Jesus' use of the Targumic tradition can be related to the question of his stance towards the law overall, since any Targum would have been understood in its own time to be a part of the written and interpreted revelation of God to his people. As Robert Banks has shown (1975, p. 242), there is a tendency to see Jesus' attitude towards the law as either profoundly conservative or essentially radical. The first solution is inadequate because as a simple matter of fact Jesus did on occasion break the law in respect of such basic matters as keeping the sabbath. Banks points out (pp. 242-243) that there is no indication that Jesus made a distinction along the lines of the moral rather than the ceremonial role of the law, and upheld the former at the expense of the latter. Indeed, passages such as Matthew 23:2f. would suggest that Jesus considered the law a unity in this regard, just as his contemporaries did (p. 242). But the same passage, in its agreement that the scribes and Pharisees sit on Moses' seat, also militates against the notion that Jesus made a qualitative distinction between the written law (which he accepted) and the oral law (which he abrogated). Banks sometimes argues as if this distinction were valid (pp. 237-238), but in the end he agrees that Jesus reacted negatively to the oral tradition only when it conflicted with his understanding of his own mission (p. 239). Moreover, the written law also, Banks acknowledges, is overruled by Jesus at various points throughout his ministry as it is presented in the Synoptic Gospels (pp. 239-241). On the other hand, Jesus did not by any means consistently reject the law of Moses, whether as written or interpreted. Somehow, both his acceptance of the common assumptions of early (and rabbinic) Judaism, and his apparent contradiction of the law are to be subsumed, says Banks, under the category "fulfillment" (p. 242).

"Fulfillment" must be the key in any discussion of the relationship between Jesus and the law in view of Matthew 5:17: this verse provides the vocabulary which the New Testament represents as that used by Jesus to express his mission in respect of the law. Banks makes the further, and telling, point that "fulfillment" is not said to take place by means of the Passion; it is through Jesus' very teaching that it is achieved (p. 242). But what precisely does Jesus do which could be said to amount to a (or the) "fulfilment" of the law? In one sense, of course, the question of how Jesus stands in relation to the law can be phrased as the question of his authority: who is it that claims to challenge the usual understanding of the law (p. 245)? Banks understandably involves the issue of Jesus' authority within a discussion of law in his teaching, but in doing so he is operating more theologically than historically. With the advantage of hindsight, those who understand Jesus as the final expression of who God is will naturally bracket the question of his relation to the law (which they will probably call the "Old Testament") within a discussion of his person. But the historian, unlike the theologian, is first of all interested in how

Jesus' contemporaries understood his claim to fulfill the law, and in what terms Jesus could have spoken with them of such fulfilment, without reference to events which had not yet happened. That is the historical question, which can sensibly be posed within or without the context of faith. Our conclusions about Jesus' use of Targumic tradition, as a particular instance of his attitude towards the "law" (given both in scripture and orally) as understood in his own time, are therefore helpful in coming to appreciate just what sort of fulfilment Jesus claimed to bring. Such a historical appreciation of Jesus' "fulfilment" is then of importance to theology, as it is the purpose of the third part of our study to develop.

Part Three

JESUS' STYLE
OF PREACHING SCRIPTURE
AS FULFILLED

In part two our inquiry was essentially a matter of reasoning from evidence of similarity between Jesus' sayings and the Targum. This consideration led us to formulate our thesis, that Jesus was familiar with interpretative tradition which is preserved in the Isaiah Targum, and that he presupposed his hearers' familiarity with this tradition. We were also able to see that there is a definite pattern manifest in Jesus' usage of such material. To observe Jesus' preaching style is itself of historical interest, but recent discussion of how we might handle biblical tradition today makes Jesus' approach to the biblical tradition of his own time all the more pertinent to contemporary theology.

Writing in the journal *Theology* for the year 1977, C. F. D. Moule observed that the Bible can hardly be used as if it spoke directly to our own modern situation. The alteration in cultural contexts from the biblical periods to our own is so enormous that it is highly exceptional that we should be addressed by a biblical book in the same way that its initial hearers or readers were. Indeed, the cultural context in which a passage is read largely determines the literary context in which it is seen, and therefore the meaning it is understood to have. For example, Isaiah 56:7 contains the famous statement, "My house will be called a house of prayer for all peoples." In the context of chapter 56 (particularly vv. 1-8), this is an assurance to non-Israelites who join themselves to the LORD that they are to have a place in Israel's sacrificial worship as active participants. Within the context of the book of Isaiah as a whole, this assurance links up with the theme that God acts through all men on behalf of Israel (cf. the designation of Cyrus, king of Persia, as the "anointed" or messiah at 45:1). From this perspective, the emphasis of the passage would seem to fall more on the all-inclusive providence of God than on the specific status of non-Israelites. Whether one looked at the narrower or at the wider context probably depended for the most part on whether one was in the cultural context of those to whom this promise was directly addressed, or in the cultural context of those to whom the book in which it was incorporated was addressed, and the interplay of these two sorts of context (literary and cultural) can be shown to have influenced the way in which this particular verse was seen in an even more radical manner.

The rabbis Simeon ben Yohai and Johanan took the phrase within the context of their Bible, the Old Testament as a whole. To them, God's promises to Israel were paramount, and therefore the meaning of the passage must be that if God can speak of non-Israelites as he does in Isaiah 56:7, his blessing will be all the greater on Israel (Shabbath 118b). Here, the Old Testament promise to Israel is taken as the normative context of the passage, and this corresponds to the interpretative orientation of rabbinic Judaism, which looked to the Bible for the ethnic focus and ethical guidance which had once been associated with king and Temple. The shifts in cultural contexts from the non-Israelite addressees of Isaiah 56, to the readers of Isaiah as a whole, and to the rabbinic interpreters of the Old Testament, are therefore evident, and serve to determine, along with the text itself, the literary context in which the passage is seen; to speak of literary context apart from cultural context as if it were an objective phenomenon is, or at least in certain circumstances may be, misleading. The force of Isaiah 56:7 will vary considerably according to the historical or cultural situation of the reader. Many Christians are probably most aware of these words as a result of their application by Jesus in the New Testament. Here again, context very much determines how one views the significance which attaches to Jesus' use of the passage. For his initial hearers, as we observed in part one, Jesus' citation was probably an attack on specific cultic innovations; but a reader of the entire New Testament— particularly if he had the epistle to the Hebrews in mind— might well take his words to imply a rejection of ritual sacrifice as a matter of principle. We therefore find that one can describe five different bibilical contexts—with five distinct concomitant meanings—for Isaiah 56:7. One's own understanding of the text is, of course, also influenced by his own cultural and historical context, and this complicates further the biblical context in which he will see the passage. Prof. Moule's point therefore seems eminently sensible; the expectation that the Bible should address us directly is naïve.

On first sight, this observation would seem to undermine the very possibility of a biblically based faith: if the Bible does not speak to me directly, then surely my belief can have nothing to do with its belief. At this stage, we must introduce a crucial distinction. Although the Bible is possessed of any number of beliefs, many of which are simply products of the ages in which the biblical books were written, the biblical faith in one God is part of the message the preachers, tradents, authors, editors and scribes who produced the Bible wished to convey. To have a biblically based faith does not imply that one shares the precise outlook and all the beliefs of, to give two examples, Abraham and Paul. Practically no Jews accept the practice of sacrifice as Abraham did, and few Christians share Paul's low esteem for women. Properly speaking, a believing reader shares with his biblical predecessors the God of Abraham, the God of Paul, and only coincidentally does he hold other beliefs which make his outlook similar to theirs. In order to confess a biblically based faith, one must acknowledge the God of the Bible, no more and no less. That this is an absolute minimum, required of anyone who professes biblical faith (and not merely an interest in the Bible), is perhaps evident, but a word of explanation may be necessary to show why biblically based faith is also — in principle — *no more* than confessing the God of the Bible. The orientation of faith is towards God as he rules my life and my world: unless one is willing to confess God's power in such personal terms, one's assertion is at best an abstract or philosophical statement, not an expression of faith.

It may, of course, be objected that some Christians in fact use credal formulae of the type, "I believe...," more to identify themselves socially and philosophically with certain select groups than to admit that God is the source of their being and the value they strive most for. That this may be or even probably is the case in many instances may be granted (cf. Barr [1977]), but our argument is not damaged by this recognition, because our concern is not to describe what certain Christians call faith, but to define how anyone could reasonably claim to hold a biblically based faith. To acknowledge that God was worshipped by Abraham, Isaac, Jacob, Jesus and Paul, and that he was primary within their respective views of reality, does not suffice as a confession of faith, although historically it is an accurate enough statement. Similarly, I would not be doing justice to the personal commitment required in confessions of faith if I claimed merely that there are certain historical connections between me and Abraham, Isaac, Jacob, Jesus and Paul. Again, this is correct, and the historian would be foolish not to admit it in any account of the rise of Western civilization, but admitting it would not make him a believer. It follows from this observation that an attempt to identify faith with certain ancient beliefs, however noble they may be, is wide of the mark. Faith is rather an individual's *cri du coeur*, which he may discover on reflexion is also the confession of Abraham, Isaac, Jacob, Jesus and Paul. Unless a belief is both a statement of the individual's consciousness of himself in the world and at the same time an expression which is recognizably related to scriptural values, it is no evidence for a biblically based faith. From Abraham to the contemporary believer there does exist a perceivable historical continuity: from the perspective of faith, that is not material. From this point of view, the only substantive issue is whether one believes in God as Abraham believed. If so, one is — in Paul's language — a son of Abraham (cf. Galatians 3:6-9). The distinction between the historical observation of what biblical faith was and the confession of such faith today is sometimes overlooked in contemporary theological discussion. In a useful volume of essays which deals largely with interpretative issues, Dennis Nineham very properly specifies what function historical observation should have within interpretation. It is a matter, he argues, of using the New Testament as evidence of the response of early Christians to Christ. (From our perspective, we would wish to broaden this description of the historical programme in order more conveniently to include the Old Testament. Basically, however, the understanding of history which Nineham defends is accepted in the present study.) Nineham's formulation of the historical task enables him to disabuse his readers of the idea that the only job the historian has is to decide whether a given incident in the New Testament happened just as it is related (1977, pp. 89-90). Whether or not a narrative in the Bible corresponds to our own view of history to such an extent that we can be confident that it speaks to us as a modern reporter would, it conveys a message which should be understood in its own terms. As we saw in the introduction to part two, the historian is sometimes pressed by his sources to suspend his conventional assumptions of what is possible in the natural world. In the case of exorcisms allegedly performed by Jesus, he must at least acknowledge that Jesus' contemporaries thought they happened, whatever we might have thought had we been there at the time with our own modern perceptions of reality. We must speak of the sources in such cases as evidencing the response to Jesus, not as yielding immediately historical information about Jesus. Under scrutiny, exorcism stories might manifest such historical information, but their consistent or primary purpose is not historical. In an autobiographical remark (p. 106) Nineham suggests that his more mature understanding of history in the Bible enabled him to overcome a certain narrowness in his background. Earlier, his concern was so taken up with how much in the New Testament actually happened or, at least, could have happened, that he failed to pay attention to the wealth of material which speaks eloquently of the response to Jesus. Only his maturing understanding of history enabled him, and may enable us, to appreciate the New Testament on its own terms as a book of confessing faith, not a punctilious chronicle (p. 90). The intellectual development of which Nineham speaks is of immediate importance to a great number, perhaps the majority, of Christians. Given our understanding of how the world works, much in the Bible strikes us as incredible, and so we ask, "Did it actually happen?" That question is important, because it makes a difference to how we view a narrative if the narrator was speaking of something he thought really happened, and if he was correct in his opinion. But our comparison of some New Testament material to rabbinic haggadoth shows that some stories were valued in the early Church more for their theological content than for their historicity. Some haggadoth are historical and some are not, but all are illustrative of truths (some of a historical nature) valued by the storyteller. From our modern perspective, the question "Did it really happen?" is probably unavoidable, and the pretence that what actually occurred does not matter is less than totally honest. On the other hand, the fact that we have for reasons of integrity to put the question of historicity does not mean we can always answer it. Sometimes we can answer only obliquely (as in the exorcism story we discussed), or not at all (as, I would say, in the case of the precise events surrounding Jesus' birth). Nonetheless, there remains a great deal to be said in respect of the sort of material we are dealing with and what it was designed to convey. Nineham's case for this position is most convincing, and attractively constructed.

The difficulty with Nineham's position is that he moves so quickly from his view of biblical history to his evaluation of the significance of that history as to suggest he confuses the two. Having appreciated the historical character of the New Testament as that of evidence regarding the disciples' response to Jesus, Nineham goes on to assert that this response is in itself part of "the saving event" (pp. 90-91). The last phrase is vague, but in using it Nineham would seem to mean that God once did something in the past which even now offers the prospect of "salvation." In so expressing himself, he aligns his thinking with the approach of the salvation history school, according to which certain historical events in the Bible are held to be revelations of God. As James Barr has shown (1980, pp. 10-11), this approach suffers from the basic difficulty that the Bible is not a book of history. Just at this point, it might be argued that Nineham provides a way forward: "history" is to be understood as the historical reactions of disciples and others, not as the people and events to which the Bible makes reference. In fact, a formulation such as Nineham's would justify the characterization of the New Testament (and, suitably modified, of the Bible as a whole) as "history." But there is no justification at this stage for saying that this biblical "history" in any sense amounts to "salvation." Nineham seems simply to assume that the Bible attests and conveys the "saving event," and because he comes to understand that "history" can be found in the Bible only in a qualified way, he equates this qualified understanding of biblical history with salvation. The question he does not answer is: why should we think the Bible attests and conveys "the saving event" in the first place?

To his credit, Nineham openly states that he *assumes* that God has acted in history in order to save the world (pp. 65-66). It is on the strength of this assumption that he can claim that the very response to this activity has the character of inspiration (p. 66, cf. pp. 88, 155). But what exactly is the strength of this assumption? As an assumption, the statement "God acts in history" is scarcely permissible. The nature of the definition of "God" is such that the word cannot be applied hypothetically: "God" refers to the creator of all that is, and ascribes a personal status to this creator. The use of the word in itself is daring. Neutrally, I can say as a historian, "Paul believed in God." But I cannot say, "I believe in God" with anything like objective detachment. The latter statement is a considerable confession, one which asserts that I know a personal creator of the universe well enough to trust him. This is not a matter of assumption or of theory, but of commitment: I either believe or I do not. Statements of trust can only be made on a reasonable basis once one has experience or knowledge of the object in whom one puts one's trust. Trust is not a matter, in the nature of the case, of logical proof: I trust a friend, for example, because my intimacy with him leads me to do so, but I can have no strictly logical proof of what he is about to do in the matter I have entrusted to him. My friendship with him does not enable me to control or even entirely to predict what he in his autonomy will do. On the other hand, I do not genuinely trust anyone on mere assumption. In any personal matter, some intimacy generally precedes trust (although trust may then produce further intimacy). Even the conventional courtesies we normally exchange and rely on for ordinary and daily meetings with people are withheld if we think we are dealing with someone, for example a man with a weapon on a deserted street at night-time, who does not belong to the circle defined by the observation of such civility. If trust in ordinary experience is not a matter of assumption, then the language of assumption, hypothesis and theory should not be used in the description of faith in God, which is largely a matter of trust.

Nineham's use of the language of assumption in describing faith is no mere lapse: he elsewhere defines his own stance as essentially the product of his upbringing and his continuing experience in the Christian community (p. 107). It is for this reason that the question of the origin of the community is so crucial for him. If the community derives its tradition from the "saving event," then the assumption of that tradition is obviously justified (p. 107). In stating the case in this way, Nineham has performed an important service for contemporary discussion. He has shown that for him the question of Christian origins is not only tied up with the question of faith: the issue of origins is in itself the question of faith. Put crudely, if he accepts Christian tradition, and Christian tradition derives ultimately from "the Christ-event," then he knows he believes in God. That may seem a circuitous route to faith, but Nineham has charted a path followed by many Christians. The plethora of journals, books, records and cassettes about the Bible which today is available to readers at almost every educational level witnesses a conscious need for some kind of proof that the faith is true. What counts as proof varies from reader to reader. For a fundamentalist, it will need to consist of a demonstration that the Bible inerrantly reports on events which happened precisely as it says it did. For a liberal who is taken by "salvation history," proof will be of a somewhat different nature: it will consist of the demonstration that the Bible evidences the response to key "saving events," such as the ministry of Jesus and the exodus from Egypt. Fundamentalists and liberals of this sort regularly and sometimes rudely indulge in fierce debates about the sort of history the Bible evidences, but both groups accept without discussion that their own versions of "history" (fundamentalist or liberal) provide the keystone of faith. Everything for them depends on the continuity of their particular traditions with the Bible's reference to events which they say reveal God. In the end, faith is a matter of history for both groups, but different sorts of history.

Again, what is most immediately striking about such a route to faith is its circuity. At the end of the tortuous path, however, one has certain events which, it is claimed, reveal God. The long battle about whether these events took place and how they are reported in the Bible, a battle in which fundamentalists and liberals appear never to tire, often obscures the fact that to call an event "saving" (or "revelatory," or the like) is not a historical judgment at all. A historian can, and often must, assert that people in the past believed God had saved them by doing certain things. But, in the nature of his discipline, he cannot claim as a historical judgment that, for example, God brought Israel out of Egypt. Because that is the case, it is not of immediately theological interest whether the sea parted by miraculous means or the world was completely made in a week. What is of immediately theological interest is this: when I read the passages of the Bible which speak of these things, whether as chronicle, legend, poem, song, prayer or whatever, do I or do I not recognize the God I trust in my own experience? That is the issue of faith, more precisely, of a biblically based faith. It cannot be equated with the question of the sort of history we are dealing with in the Bible, nor does this question even address the issue of faith directly. One is not any more a believer because he holds the sea parted as dramatically as in the special effects of the Hollywood rendering of the exodus, nor any less so because he thinks Darwin might have a point after all. The issue of faith is that of whether I perceive and respond to God as I read the Bible, of whether I am—in Pauline language—a son of Abraham.

Indeed, the situation, grounded as it is on the analogy of faith between biblical documents and ourselves, is itself of Pauline dimensions, in that—behind the individual historical questions, which must attend a critical reading of the Bible—the essential question it poses is that of the revelation "of faith to faith" (Romans 1:17). When Paul used this phrase in his letter to the Romans, he did so to insist that God's "righteousness," the very power of God in the preaching (cf. v. 16), has been revealed to both Jews and Greeks, despite the differences that divided them. The quality he calls "faith" is to his thinking already designated as the central issue by the prophets (above all, in Habakkuk 2:4, cf. Romans 1:17) and is, as we have remarked, the basis of believers' claim to kinship with Abraham. Despite the cultural discontinuity between Jew and Greek, or better, precisely in the light of this discontinuity, the power of God is for Paul manifest in the unity of faith among believers. The claim Paul makes about the solidarity between Jewish and

Gentile believers is essentially of the same order as his claim about the relationship between Abraham and his "sons," and corresponds to one's assertion today that one's God is the God of the Bible. The difficulty with such claims about the continuity of faith is that they frequently seem to be entirely subjective. How can I say that my faith is the same as that of a person living in a cultural milieu different from my own? Even if he agrees this is the case, we may be speaking of different things when we refer to "God," "faith," "redemption," etc. Were I speaking to a person who came from an Islamic culture, the name "Jesus Christ" is likely for him to carry associations so different from those it carries for me that a discussion about faith will be impossible. The still current reluctance to speak of religion at a formal gathering perhaps reflects an anxious awareness that agreed social conventions will not stretch to describing the contents of faith, even among people of similar backgrounds. If we have such difficulties in relating our faith to our contemporaries, how can we possibly join Paul in the claim that together we share an affinity with Abraham's faith?

As long as "faith" is understood in a purely individualistic way, discussion and agreement on what it is will be impossible. On the other hand, such an understanding of faith is probably a result — at least to a certain extent — of our experience of religious diversity in the West. After the wars of religion, the toleration of differences was, politically and humanly speaking, the only way forward. By the eighteenth century, extermination had been tried (as in the case of the Huguenots in France), various forms of partition had been tried (as in the American colonies), comprehensive state religion had been tried (as in the Church of England); morally and practically, such solutions threw up insurmountable problems. Toleration, with the understanding that individual conscience should determine one's religious affiliation, presented itself gradually as the best available political option. But experience has taught us that this option also has its limitations. As long as there is some moral affinity among the religious systems people choose, they can tolerate — if not approve — one another's choices. But it only requires the Jonestown suicides or the Manson killings to remind us that what we call "faith" can lead to socially unacceptable behaviour, and that toleration is only possible in the framework of agreed values. Politically speaking, then, a purely individualistic understanding of faith is inadequate. Theologically, it is positively misleading. The assertion, "I believe in God," is certainly one which only the individual can make for himself, but precisely because "God" is the object of his faith, his assertion is not just a personal opinion. "God," by definition, is not just my private ideal; if he is God at all, he in some way must be active in the world as its creator, and evident in the experience of others. My faith is therefore only true to its object when I attempt to relate what I believe to what others believe. That is not to say that my faith is validated by what others believe, only that any retreat from dialogue is tantamount to an admission that one's "faith" is in fact a purely personal matter. The search for *correlation* — which is far different from validation or compromise — is a characteristic of faith in God: it evidences the sincerity of the belief that God in some way rules the world in which we live.

The search for correlation, a necessary concomitant of faith, drives the individual into dialogue, and ultimately into a community defined by its members' dialogue with one another. They will speak to one another, read, sing, pray and worship together, and more, all because the faith of the one desires correlation with that of the others. Those communities which confess a biblically based faith also use such activities to explore their commonly held views, but their distinguishing feature is their use of the Bible. They make this book their manual for discussing faith, and therefore seek correlation from the past as well as the present. The tendencies towards community and continuity with tradition are shared by many religious faiths; the uniqueness of biblically based faith lies precisely in the Bible itself, and its success depends on the Bible's appeal. Without the individual's conviction that the Bible brings his own faith to expression and enables him, with others, to see what it means to believe in God and live in the world, any claim that his faith is biblically based must seem empty.

The Bible is therefore the focus of a certain community of faith, a community of contemporaries who claim continuity with a long tradition. As Prof. Moule's article suggests, however, this document, even though it is of supreme importance to the members of the community as the expression and standard of their faith, should not be thought to replace faith. Rather, the Bible guides the search for correlation among those who use it as their standard, if it is used with the understanding that they believe actively and are not just passive recipients of the expressions of past generations of faith. To put the matter simply: the Bible does not provide us directly with answers to our theological or ethical questions, but informs our faith, which is able to contribute such answers. This appraisal of the situation does not involve any special claims for the power of faith: what an individual puts his trust in, be it God, himself, an ideal, money, etc., does largely determine how he thinks and behaves. In one sense, everyone is a believer; the question is merely what he believes in. If he says, "I believe and trust in God as he is revealed in the Bible," he has answered that question in a way which identifies him with a certain community and tradition.

Faith is a distinctively human faculty. Our lives in society are defined to a great extent by what we think is most valuable, by what we trust and by what beliefs we choose to act on. Even to disclaim belief makes a positive statement on the relative value of personal doubt as compared to traditional doctrine, and shows that the speaker cherishes his individual reason more than the community whose teaching he rejects. His actions preach faith in the individual, albeit a doubt-torn individual. No matter what we do or refuse to do, we must at any given moment decide on behalf of one thing over another, and this decision is usually evident to those around us, and becomes, in turn, one factor in their faith-decisions. Seen in this context, to confess a biblically based faith does not involve a believer in a decision which is out of the ordinary, but implies only that one has taken up a specific option in the course of making an essentially human decision.

For a believer (using the term as commonly understood), then, the Bible is what brings his faith to expression; Prof. Moule speaks of it as evidencing the "Christ-event" and bringing us "to Jesus Christ." This is a shorthand way of saying the Bible brings us to faith in Jesus Christ, and perhaps — if we wish to speak of the Bible as a whole, and not only or primarily of the New Testament — it would be better to speak of the Bible as orienting our faith in God. Such faith includes Jesus for those who accept the New Testament as part of the Bible, while those who read only the Old Testament as biblical will wish to express their faith in a different way. The issue Prof. Moule points to remains the same: how do we get from the Bible to religious faith? For the believer, this issue is obviously crucial, and, for two reasons, even non-believers should not ignore it. First, their own faith-decisions — whatever they may be — might be illuminated by an understanding of how one comes to a biblically based faith. Second, the faith mechanism of Jews and Christians is of historical and cultural importance. It would therefore be narrow in a work of the present kind not to consider our results from the point of view of the more general question: how does one — in the light of Jesus' practice — come to a faith which is consonant with the Bible?

The very fact that such a question can be put and, in all honesty, must be put, evidences a profound difficulty in contemporary theology. At least since the Enlightenment, theology has accepted the methods of historical disciplines, and within the field of biblical studies the paramount issues have been, "what did the author actually mean?" and "what actually happened?" As Peter Stuhlmacher has recently suggested in a history of biblical interpretation (1979, cf. R. M. Grant [1972]), this historical bias contributed a certain precision to theological thinking, but it is no replacement for theological thinking as a whole. Only after one has understood both a writer and his background can one address the specifically theological question: is the author's statement about God true? A historical approach obviously helps us to specify what we think an author means, but it is no method for deciding whether or to what extent he is right. In order to address this difficulty, Stuhlmacher calls for a fresh approach to the Bible according to what he calls "the hermeneutics of consent." By this he means that the reader of the Bible is invited to "consent" to the biblical picture of God as a description of God in his own experience. This is precisely what we understand by the less technical phrase "biblically based faith," and our question, "how does one come to believe in what one reads?" is rather similar to his, "how does one consent to the hermeneutical picture offered by the Bible?"

The methods of historical reconstruction, then, are only the appropriate vehicle for a certain approach to the Bible. They are designed to help us to see what people said under what circumstances. The vehicle has been at our doorstep for two centuries, and we have learned its peculiarities. We know the roads that are best for it; it is suited for scenic cruising on the lowlands of the Bible, and from that perspective we can better appreciate the mountainous proportions of Jesus and the faith which grew up around him. But it is one thing to appreciate the vastness of the highlands, quite another to ascend them. Methods of historical reconstruction can help to describe the faith of those who contributed to the New Testament, but in themselves their function is not to make a statement of faith on the basis of the New Testament. Historical discussion might well, and often has, formed the occasion for theological discussion, but the first does not take the place of the second, any more than knowing about Jesus takes the place of believing in him. Knowledge may be for some a path to faith, but knowledge and faith are obviously not the same thing.

If — as we have argued, and has been a matter of conventional wisdom since the time of Martin Kähler (1896) — historical criticism and the literary disciplines associated with it are not the equivalent of believing, does that mean we can do without them? A recent book by Gerhard Maier answers "yes"; it is portentously entitled, *The End of the*

Historical-Critical Method (1977). This book is representative of a strong trend in recent discussion towards a criticism which does not pose historical questions. The trend is supported by those (of whom Maier is an example) who are convinced that history is not a certain means to faith and by those who wish to see the Bible purely as a specimen of literature, regardless of its historical value. The latter strand of the movement is represented by David Gunn (1978), who argues that 2 Samuel can be understood by taking it simply as a "story." Unquestionably, a dogmatically historical preoccupation has in the past led to a neglect of the literary patterns and themes which are crucial to the understanding of the book. But if I am to understand the author's work, it is surely important that I have some notion of whether or not he has relied on earlier material in respect of David, and whether or not he saw that material as historically valuable. Without such an understanding, we cannot appreciate the nature of his work. No doubt, the author did not have our critical view of history; that is the product of the Enlightenment, and reflects the concern of the period to weed out the quantity of medieval documents which had been treated as historical sources, but were in fact forgeries (cf. Lonergan [1973] pp. 175-234). In the face of writings designed to deceive, one's attitude becomes understandably suspicious, and one's method rather more rigorous; the author of 2 Samuel almost certainly had a different attitude to the traditions he drew upon. Nonetheless, it makes a difference to our understanding of the meaning of his work to know whether he thought what he says happened actually did happen, and it makes a difference to our evaluation of the significance of his work to know whether what he says happened in fact occurred.

Our historical way of seeing things, including our suspicion that the sources might trick us, is — lamentably or not — just part of our approach to the world around us. To suspend it when we deal with the Bible would be unnatural, and would deny us the possibilty of knowing it as we know other things. Just because a repression of our natural desire for historical knowledge arbitrarily limits the possibilities of our knowledge as a whole, such a repression is also undesirable from the point of view of faith. If believing in God involves my whole orientation to the world in which I find myself, then my way of seeing God should be at least as accurate as my usual way of seeing the world. If it is anything less, if religious knowledge is only a fraction of ordinary knowledge, the suspicion arises that what is called faith is really only an incomplete, perhaps escapist, way of looking at the world. Within the context of biblical faith in particular, to say one's God is the God of Abraham, Isaac, Jacob, Jesus and Paul, and then to admit of no historical interest in who those people were, is surely a nonsense. What makes faith biblical is precisely its identification with the ways the Bible speaks of God, and to understand that involves ordinary historical inquiry. Faith cannot be reduced to ordinary historical knowledge, but such knowledge is normally included in faith.

Historical criticism, then, has clear limitations, and by itself is no substitute for faith or theological discourse. But as a vehicle for appreciating the Bible and the forms of faith it reflects, it will do many more miles of service; the old banger should not yet be traded in. Because we largely perceive the past in historical terms, it is unsatisfying and evasive not to pose historical questions about the Bible and try to answer those questions. Precisely because the Bible is a corpus of documents from antiquity, nothing less than a historically grounded approach to it can serve our critical faculty. But the dissatisfaction experienced by Maier, and by many others, with historical critical treatments of the Bible is understandable. From the time of the second German edition of Karl Barth's commentary on Romans (1921), twentieth century theologians have been attempting, in Barth's words, "to see through and beyond history into the spirit of the Bible, which is the Eternal Spirit" (1933, p. 1). But the desire to slice through history in this way, unless it is guided by a critical method, will look suspiciously like a literalistic approach to the Bible, which suspends normal criteria of judgment just because an allegedly holy book is the topic of inquiry. As we have seen, the character of faith is such that it cannot rest easy when its foundation is an unjustified suspension of ordinary intelligence. The issues involved in relating the scriptures to faith, and vice versa, are therefore complex, and reach to the heart of what it means to believe. A consideration of Jesus' usage of the Old Testament in his preaching is therefore theologically significant, even though one's approach to it must, in the first instance, be historical.

In our conclusion to part two, we observed that Jesus did not use Targumic tradition in such a way that his teaching constituted an express citation of it. In the case of his reference to "the kingdom of God," Jesus presents himself as speaking and acting on behalf of a God who is disclosing himself for the sake of his people. God's personal intervention is depicted more vividly and realistically by Jesus than it is in the Targum, and it is held to be revealed by him in a more immediate way. Accordingly, Jesus actively sent others to promulgate his message about the kingdom, and healed in its name, while in the Targum the kingdom is only discussed by way of exegetical consideration. There is an important difference between Jesus and the Targum here which has nothing to do with the relative degree of nationalism in each of the two; for reasons we have seen, a distinction along the lines of nationalism is not tenable. The significant and obvious dissimilarity is that Jesus preaches as a matter of experience what the Targum mentions by way of explicit reflexion on the biblical text. The two assertions about the kingdom are practically identical in their reference to God's saving activity on behalf of his people, but the contexts of their respective assertions are crucially distinctive. What is said in the Targum pertains to the deliverance promised within scripture; Jesus speaks of our present experience, or of our experience as it soon will be, as a function of "the kingdom of God." Jesus, then, seems to have proceeded on the basis of the popular understanding of the Old Testament; his Bible, for the purposes of preaching, was what his audience understood as the Bible. In the course of this investigation, we have not uncovered a single instance in which Jesus seemed arbitrarily to have departed from the

Targumic interpretation available in his day. On the other hand, he seems to have adapted the Targumic kingdom theology so that it became a vehicle for speaking of what God is doing in experience. For this reason, although there are definite connections between Jesus and the Isaiah Targum in the matter of the kingdom, the dominical kingdom sayings are certainly not citations of the Targum. "The kingdom of God" becomes in Jesus' preaching an experiential category. Building on vocabulary shared with the biblical interpretation of the synagogue, his kingdom sayings —particularly the parables — offer a view of God as king which they challenge the hearer to accept within the terms and conditions of his own experience.

The relationship between Jesus and the Targumic tradition of his day permits us to speak more exactly about the relationship between the Old Testament and the New Testament than an entirely general comparison would allow. In a recent survey of modern discussion of the relationship between the two Testaments, David Baker (1976) has shown the difficulty of expressing the significance of the Bible without exalting one Testament at the expense of the other. Most modern Christians, encouraged by lectionaries currently in use, refer to the New Testament as their Bible for practical purposes, almost to the exclusion of the Old Testament. Israel's religion — along with Judaism — is frequently seen as a legalistic system whose only value is to highlight the value of the new dispensation. This entire perspective has been discredited during the course of the present study. A more sophisticated subordination of the Old Testament to the New Testament involves the contention that the former provides promises which actually (some would say literally) achieve fulfilment only in the New Testament. As Baker points out (p. 373), the difficulty with this solution is that there is more to the New Testament than the fulfilment of traditional expectations. In the specific case of Jesus' use of Targumic tradition, we have seen instances in which not merely the Old Testament, but specifically early Jewish interpretation of the Old Testament, provides the substance of New Testament teaching. There is no question of the Old Testament being superceded or "fulfilled" (in the sense used above) in these instances: Jesus seems rather to have used the tradition available to him positively, in order to articulate his message. One obviously cannot generalize about the overall relationship between the Testaments on the limited evidence we have considered in respect of Jesus; on the other hand, no general account which ignores such evidence could be said to be satisfactory.

Because Jesus used the biblical interpretative tradition of his time in a positive way, it is accurate to say that his preaching represents a further interpretation of that tradition. "The kingdom of God," for example, is applied within experience, rather than exegesis, and so acquires fresh meaning. Or again, Isaiah's description of dull-witted listeners is applied to Jesus' own hearers. In these cases — indeed, in all the cases we have discussed in part two which pertain to Jesus directly — our appreciation of Jesus' preaching is enhanced by knowing and considering the tradition on which he relied. As a matter of fact, in some instances such an appreciation is only possible on the basis of this knowledge. The present study illustrates specifically the general principle that one cannot understand Jesus without reference to the early Judaism which nurtured him and which provided the context of his preaching.

In the survey we have already mentioned, Baker (1976) rightly rejects the contention that the New Testament is simply an interpretation (or even, the necessary interpretation) of the Old Testament (p. 365). As we have seen, to understand Jesus necessarily involves an awareness of the interpretative element of his preaching. But to say that does not imply that he (much less the New Testament as a whole) provides only, or even primarily, an interpretation of the Old Testament. In fact, a substantively new element appears to be present in the New Testament as compared to the Old. But what is this element? Baker himself refers to the ministry of Jesus (p. 365), and much the same thing is said by James Barr in the context of identifying the essentially new element in the New Testament (1980, p. 128). At one level, of course, it is difficult to fault this sort of statement: the New Testa-

ment as a whole can be said to refer to Jesus Christ as a
divine event in a way the Old Testament does not. It is
almost a truism to speak of Jesus as the substantively fresh
subject matter of the New Testament. Actually, however, if
Jesus and his followers intended principally to interpret
scripture, then even this apparently fresh element in the New
Testament is in fact partially derivative from the Old Testament. Again, what we have done in this volume would not
provide an adequate basis for a complete investigation of
this possibility, but we can at least see how Jesus used
biblical interpretative tradition. His use of the scripture as
understood in his day might reasonably influence our use of
scripture as understood in ours, and also our apprehension
of the relationship betwen the Testaments.

In describing Jesus' characteristic use of the Targumic
tradition of his time, restraint is required so as not to make it
seem a rule or principle, or even a norm, for all preaching.
There is no straightforward evidence that Jesus was concerned to develop a systematic method of interpreting the
scripture. Although Jesus' style of interpretation was disturbing to many of his contemporaries, it was precisely
those who were most rigid in their own approach to the
Bible who were most nonplussed at Jesus.

The Pharisees confidently say, for example, that Jesus'
disciples break the law by plucking grain on the sabbath,
only to receive the reply that there is a similarity between
David and Jesus, and that this connection authorizes their
action, because David's followers also acted in an unusual
way in respect of the cult (Matthew 12:1-8; Mark 2:23-28;
Luke 6:1-5). In this case, the regular reading of the Old
Testament as a book of ethical instruction, championed by
the Pharisees, clashes with Jesus' less systematic interpretation, which is flexible enough to take account of an exceptional factor (viz. his relation to David).

Similarly, the attempt is made by the Sadducees to prove
from the law that Jesus' teaching about the resurrection is
foolish. Because, they argue, Moses made provision for a
man to raise up children with his brother's wife if his brother
died childless, there must be no resurrection, since in a

resurrected state the woman would have more than one husband (Matthew 22:23-33; Mark 12:18-27; Luke 20:27-38). Jesus' reply again appeals to exceptional circumstances in the case, which he claims his opponents do not deal adequately with: resurrection is not just a continuation of human relations as we know them, and marriage in particular is not perpetuated (Matthew 22:30; Mark 12:25; Luke 20:35, 36). Moreover, he goes on to claim that as God is called the God of Abraham, Isaac and Jacob, these three must be understood to be alive in some sense, since otherwise God would only be a God of the dead (Matthew 22:31, 32; Mark 12:26, 27; Luke 20:37, 38). While the Sadducees' position rests on the methodical application of the law to the hypothesis that there is a resurrection, Jesus' response is more a matter of simple assertion. He claims that the resurrection is not what his opponents say it is, and this objection is completely unsupported by any argument. The appeal to Abraham, Isaac and Jacob is also scarcely a case in logic, but depends on the hearer's agreement that the living God is of such a majesty that the patriarchs who are associated with him should also be thought of as living. Someone who does not share that point of view cannot be expected to accept Jesus' counterclaim.

A last example of Jesus' conflict with those who prided themselves on a systematic interpretation will perhaps suffice to show that he himself was not inclined in that direction. In reply to the teaching of the scribes that the messiah should be thought of as David's son, a claim based firmly on the Old Testament motif of the throne which is promised to David's descendants, Jesus makes a rather complicated point (Matthew 22:41-45; Mark 12:35-37a; Luke 20:41-44). He starts from the belief of his time that David composed the book of Psalms, and cites Psalm 110, "The Lord said to my lord...," and takes it that "my lord" refers to the messiah. But, he concludes, if David calls him "my lord," then the messiah should not be thought of simply as a successor of David in the royal line (cf. Chilton [1982[2]]). The objection is clever, and rests on the popular image of David as a psalmist, but it is of the same exceptional, non-systematic nature as the examples cited above. It seems much more a style than a method, and depends largely on appeals to popular conceptions, namely of David and the resurrection. Since Jesus does not seem consciously to have promulgated a norm of preaching, it is ironic when his sayings are treated as if they provided such a norm. From the outset, we would do better to speak of the preaching style of Jesus, and to characterize that style first of all as experiential, in that categories, language and images found in the biblical tradition of his own time were taken up by Jesus as descriptions of the present activity of God.

By no stretch of the imagination, however, can Jesus be said simply to have used the Targumic interpretation of Isaiah as if it exactly represented what God was doing in his own understanding. We have already seen in part two that Jesus seems never to have cited the Targumic wording exactly; a degree of deviation from the expected diction may well have given his teaching the appeal of originality. Even when the book of Isaiah is explicitly cited in Jesus' teaching and the connection with the Targum is obvious (cf. Mark 4:11, 12), the deviation from any known traditional rendering is very striking. The citation of Isaiah 66:24 in Mark 9:48 constitutes a reference to Targumic tradition which can be described as truncated in much the same way. The abbreviation — relative to Isaiah Targum 50:11 — in Matthew 26:52 manifests a similar phenomenon in respect of Jesus' usage of proverbial material in the Targum, and the same might be said of Matthew 7:2; Mark 4:24. The usage of the idiom "mammon of deceit" at Luke 16:9 may also be a bold application of language normally associated with biblical interpretation. For that matter, the fact that Jesus used "kingdom of God" in the context of experience, not of exegesis, shows that an innovative tendency is also characteristic of his style of preaching.

The innovation evident in Jesus' preaching, however, cannot be described as undifferentiated creativity, or originality for its own sake. The language of biblical interpretation, already familiar to his hearers, is enthusiastically used by Jesus insofar as it evokes the picture of God he wishes to convey, but it is not used beyond that point. Tradition is for him a shared point of departure which unites him with his audience and permits them to share the same theological language, but it is not a strait-jacket. Such a readiness to distance oneself from the biblical text is really necessary if biblical categories are to be used to characterize present experience. When the Bible is used to describe the present position, the point at issue is how God is with us; in many other ways, our situation will obviously not be that of the biblical author. Jesus would appear to have recognized this, and accordingly he used the Targumic tradition in a critical manner, sometimes availing himself of its interpretation and its idioms, but by no means restricting himself to them. To a certain extent, of course, the apparent discrepancies between Jesus and Targumic tradition might be the result of accidental factors, as we have discussed in part two. We have immediate access neither to the Targumic tradition contemporaneous with Jesus, nor to the exact words he spoke. We know the former only through a document shaped by events unknown to Jesus, and the latter only through documents in the Greek language written (at the later stages) by people to whom the Isaiah Targum was not a revered tradition. Nonetheless, despite these difficulties — which it was the purpose of part two to overcome by critical means — the evidence consistently suggests that Jesus used the biblical interpretative tradition his hearers were familiar with and that he departed from that tradition at certain key points. Our use of the term "critical" to describe this aspect of his preaching style is not at all intended to imply that Jesus shared our own modern perspective on the Bible (or even that he was conscious of his own hermeneutical stance); that would obviously be anachronistic. But he does seem to have judged which elements of the Targumic tradition to embrace and which to leave unused, and this evaluative judgment is — in the most basic sense — "critical." At the same time, this critical approach to the Bible is really necessary if one is to use it experientially, since otherwise one will be unclear about how the biblical text relates to experience.

The story of the confession at Caesarea Philippi (Matthew 16:13-23; Mark 8:27-33; Luke 9:18-22) illustrates an approach to scripture which is both experiential and critical. Indeed, the passage as a whole plays deliberately on the identification of Jesus in scriptural terms. Jesus himself poses the question of his identity in the opening ("Who do men say I am?" in Mark), and a startling range of biblically based answers is presented by the disciples on behalf of their contemporaries. He is said to be John the Baptist, Elijah, or one of the prophets (Matthew specifies Jeremiah by way of example). The common element in these diverse understandings of Jesus is that an experiential approach to the Bible (that is, the Old Testament) is evident. This is obvious in the cases of Elijah and the prophets such as Jeremiah, and implicit in the case of John the Baptist. Within the Synoptic tradition, John is consistently portrayed in terms of and in images borrowed from the Old Testament. The mention of his public ministry begins with a citation from Isaiah, and proceeds to discuss his preaching and personal habits in a way which reminds us of prophets such as Elijah (Matthew 3:3-6; Mark 1:2-6; cf. Luke 3:1f.). Mark actually presents a mixed citation of Isaiah and Malachi by way of introduction to the ministry of John (1:2, 3), and a citation of the latter book features in Jesus' own characterization of John in Matthew (11:10) and Luke (7:27) as "a prophet and more than a prophet" (Matthew 11:9; Luke 7:26). The descriptions of John along biblical lines seem therefore to reach back to the way Jesus saw him, and the explicit statement in Gabriel's prediction to Zacharias in Luke 1:17 that his son would proceed "in the spirit and power of Elijah" is the logical development of a tendency which, on the face of things, originated with Jesus. (For a detailed description of the portrait of John in Matthew, Mark and Luke, cf. W. Wink [1968].)

Our analysis is by no means dependent on the judgment (much less, on the assumption) that the passage reflects an actual dialogue between Jesus and his disciples, but proceeds on the observation that the experiential approach to scripture, which we have already seen is evidenced in Jesus' usage of Targumic interpretation, is also apparent in what others are portrayed as saying about him in the passage. Our concern is the approach to scripture in this particular example of early Christian tradition, not the attribution of the tradition to a specific historical figure. Strikingly, the passage as it is presently available does not rest with a purely experiential approach. Jesus responds here with another question: "But who do you yourselves say I am?" (Matthew 16:15; Mark 8:29a; Luke 9:20a). The structure of a question followed by a response followed by a further question conveys just that critical attitude to the use of scripture which characterizes Jesus' reference to Targumic interpretation. The earlier identifications are not rejected, but neither are they embraced as adequate descriptions of Jesus.

We must pursue this passage to its conclusion, but before we do so, certain remarks might be made. First of all, it is striking that Jesus — according to the disciples' manner of presenting how others describe him — has been a catalyst which set off a reaction between the Bible and his contemporaries. Their experience of him has been such as to lead them to draw on their biblical memory in order to express it. The normative account of God's past dealings with his people has become the vehicle for apprehending and articulating what is happening in the case of Jesus. Even at this stage, it is perhaps not too much to say that the application of scripture experientially to describe Jesus is a root of christological teaching in the New Testament, although there is a long road to travel between Caesarea Philippi and the prologue of John, where the significance of Jesus is portrayed in creational terms borrowed from Genesis 1. The basic point is that Jesus' experiential style of preaching seems to have influenced those around him. No doubt, not all of Jesus' contemporaries saw him in biblical terms, but apparently even Herod Antipas viewed him as a new John (cf. Matthew 14:1, 2; Mark 6:14-16; Luke 9:7-9), so that it seems reasonable to suppose there was a popular response to Jesus of a nature such as the Caesarea Philippi episode reflects. Behind the seemingly backward response of the crowds there is an important development in Jesus' experiential style. Jesus, especially in his witness to the kingdom, claimed that scripture refers to divine activity in the present, God's own intervention on behalf of his people. His sympathetic hearers seem here not only to accept this claim, but to describe Jesus himself by means of an experiential recourse to scripture: this man who — as it were — speaks on God's behalf *is* Elijah, Jeremiah, one of the prophets, John. At this early stage, albeit in a primitive fashion, Jesus the preacher is on the way to becoming the content of preaching, and precisely because his own style of interpretation was appropriated by others.

The large number of names applied to Jesus in the New Testament, such as "lord," "son of God," "the son of man," "son of David," "prophet," "word," "king," "messiah," "rabbi," "high priest," suggests that the attempt to identify Jesus flourished and continued in essentially biblical terms. The theology of the "word" in the prologue of John, which has already been mentioned, is a prominent but characteristic fruit of this activity, and Justin Martyr was later to pursue this line of thought still further, so as to relate the "word" of creation in Christ to the "word" of reason which the creation gives to men (cf. Barnard [1967] pp. 85-100). Paul also attempted to describe Jesus by means of images borrowed from the Old Testament. In 1 Corinthians 10, Paul refers to a "spiritual rock" from which "our fathers" drank in the time of Moses (v. 4). Twice in the Pentateuch (Exodus 17:6; Numbers 20:11) God is said to have brought water miraculously forth from a rock by the agency of Moses. In popular thinking, the same rock was held to have provided this support, and so to have followed Israel through the wilderness. Paul seems aware of just these traditions, which are also available from Rabbinica, because he speaks of the rock as "following" Moses' band (cf. McNamara [1972] pp. 73, 89). "The rock," Paul goes on to say, "was Christ." In an almost off-hand way, then, Paul speaks of the supportive presence of Jesus through a very unusual biblical image and in terms of the understanding of that image in his own time.

In a similar way, he points out that the promises spoken

to Abraham in Genesis 13:15 (cf. 17:8 and 24:7) are for his "seed," not for his "seeds," and he uses this observation to refer the promise to Christ specifically (Galatians 3:16; cf. Wilcox [1979]). Within the logic of Genesis, of course, the issue of Abraham's seed is crucial, in that it seems unlikely — even impossible (cf. Genesis 15:1-6) — that he will have an heir through Sarah his wife. Paul is very well familiar with this motif; he actually cites Genesis 15:6, a key passage for his argument, in the same chapter of Galatians (v. 6), and refers explicitly to Isaac in chapter four (vv. 22-31) as the true son who will inherit (quoting Genesis 21:10 in v. 30). Isaac, as the seed of Abraham, is in chapter three an image of Christ while in chapter four he is, as the child of the promise and the son of the free woman (cf. vv. 28, 30), the image of all believers. In neither application does Paul entirely lose sight of Isaac's place in Genesis as the seed of Abraham and the son of Sarah, but he is more interested in the light Isaac casts on Jesus and the believer, and shifts the image from one to the other with a characteristic flexibility of mind. This flexibility may seem strange to us, but in the present case it shows that Paul does not make a hard and fast connection between Isaac and Christ or Isaac and believers, but wishes to use the Old Testament creatively —or, as we have said, experientially — to describe what he feels the theological situation is.

The application of the Old Testament which we have described seems to accord with the style of Jesus, unusual though it may seem to us. Because it is unusual, some scholars have found it necessary to postulate modes of thought very different from our own in order to explain it. So, for example, Anthony Hanson has suggested that, when Paul said what he did in 1 Corinthians 10:4, early Christians understood that Jesus had actually been active in the time of Moses (1965, pp. 10-25). Such arguments are at least worth considering, because it is often misleading to suppose that what we call common sense is consistent from generation to generation or from century to century: many things which were once considered sensible may now appear very odd and esoteric. Nonetheless, the consistency with which the

New Testament writers speak of Jesus as a historical figure, whose time on earth was limited chronologically, makes it seem odd to suppose that he is for them a timeless person (cf. Stanton [1974]), and we would require some indication that they systematically promulgated such a claim before the hypothesis could be considered tenable. We have, in fact, already seen that Paul's usage of the Old Testament is too flexible to suggest that he wished to make a programmatic claim to the effect that Jesus lived in the time of Moses (much less before), so that Prof. Hanson's suggestion seems questionable. Without denying that Jesus was a person whose significance for the Church could be expressed in supra-historical terms, we would suggest that no consistent doctrine of Jesus' pre-existence is expressed by the application to him of passages, terms and images from the Old Testament. Rather, the Church referred to the Old Testament in order to express the significance of Jesus, and in this sense carried on something of the experiential style of Jesus' preaching.

A critical approach to scripture is a necessary corollary to an experiential style of preaching. When one begins — as Jesus did — with an experience of God in biblical terms, one needs to be discerning in the use of those terms. Otherwise, one falls into an unproductive biblicism in which scriptural language is used for its own sake, without reference to the experienced reality of God. The structure of the Caesarea Philippi episode, together with Jesus' discerning use of Targumic tradition, suggests that Jesus had a sense of the limits of applying biblical language, and that he conveyed this sense to his followers. Because the latter point has been our focus in the discussion above, we have not had to discuss the historicity of the Caesarea Philippi episode, but only the attitude towards scripture implicit in the structure of an influential story told in the early Church. In that part of the story we have so far discussed, no Old Testament model of Jesus is offered which is explicitly rejected, but neither is any of them openly embraced. Old Testament usage is not presented as providing an unchangeable itinerary for Jesus, as if everything in scripture had to find its place in what he did and said. Scripture gives an insight into what God is doing in the present, and it is applied by Jesus and his followers with this critical attitude in mind. In so doing, they acknowledged both the value of the Bible in helping to describe God, and the freedom of God himself, who is not limited in his activity by what the Bible says of him.

The story of Caesarea Philippi goes considerably further. Peter responds to Jesus' second question with the acknowledgement, "You are the christ." It is commonly claimed that "messiah" (or "christ") in early Judaism referred to a Davidic military figure from whom the redemption of Israel was expected. In the *Psalms of Solomon* (chapter 17) a Davidic king is spoken of who is predicted to be in full authority over Israel, but his specifically military attributes are not mentioned, and his campaign to achieve power is not described. More importantly, we know of messianic expectations which were not at all to the same effect. The reference to Cyrus the Persian in Isaiah 45:1 has already been cited, and — although it is unusual, even within the universalism of the book — the conception of messiahship there is obviously not as nationalistic as might be anticipated. The writings discovered near the Dead Sea employ the term "messiah" in respect of the leadership of Israel, and also in respect of priestly leadership. The range of the usage of this term is so wide, in fact, that it seems unwarranted to imagine that a specific expectation attaches to it; etymologically, the word simply means "anointed," that is, someone designated or appointed by God. The scope of the divine commission a "messiah" might be thought to have would depend on the context in which he was called "anointed."

It is notable, in this connection, that Jesus specifies scribal messianic expectation when he queries the relation between David and the messiah (Mark 12:35; Luke 20:41; cf. v. 39 and Matthew 22:41, 42), and that when the high priest asks Jesus whether he is the messiah, he immediately explains the use of the term by adding the qualification, "the son of God" (Matthew 26:63). (The wording in Mark 14:61 amounts to offering the same qualification, while in form the tradition in Luke 22:67, 70 also presents a close associa-

tion between "messiah" and "son of God.") This confirms
the supposition that "messiah" requires some sort of explanation if it is to be used at all precisely (cf. M. de Jonge
[1966]). It is therefore not surprising that Jesus does not
reject the term as a description of himself, and yet at the
same time warns the disciples not to speak further on the
subject (Matthew 16:20; Mark 8:30; Luke 9:21). Peter is
especially praised in Matthew for saying Jesus is the messiah, but it is notable that in this Gospel the words "son of
the living God" qualify Peter's meaning (16:16), and in any
case Jesus is here portrayed explicitly as forbidding the
disciples to say that he is the messiah (16:20). When Jesus
then goes on, in Matthew and Mark, to say he must suffer,
die and rise again as the son of man, Peter's reaction shows
that, whatever he understood by "messiah" when he applied
it to Jesus, Jesus thought of himself in other terms.

The "son of man" — used by Jesus himself — is the last
identification of Jesus offered in the passage. Unfortunately, its exact meaning is far from straightforward; even
within the New Testament itself, people are portrayed as
asking the vexed question, "Who is this son of man?" (John
12:34). After the passage under discussion, the son of man
appears as a heavenly figure of vindication and judgment
(Matthew 16:27; Mark 8:38; Luke 9:26), and this may well
remind us of what we read in the seventh chapter of the book
of Daniel (vv. 13, 24), where the coming of the son of man is
associated with the ascendancy of the "saints of the most
high" (v. 27). But the suffering of the son of man is not
mentioned here, nor is this a prominent aspect of the use of
the phrase "son of man" in the book of Ezekiel, where it is
used to address the prophet. It does seem probable that
Aramaic usage might help us to understand the expression
as used by Jesus; in that language, "son of man" can be used
as a periphrasis for "I," and is more specifically associated
with the assertion that man is mortal (cf. C. F. D. Moule
[1977] pp. 11-22; J. W. Bowker [1977]). While research in
this area—which proceeds at a remarkable rate—has laid bare
some of the lineaments of meaning which may lie behind
Jesus' use of the phrase, a single exact parallel has yet to be

found. The conclusion seems reasonable that Jesus applied a somewhat out of the way phrase to himself, and gave it fresh meaning.

Within the pattern of the Caesarea Philippi passage as a whole, the significance of Jesus' use of "son of man" language seems clear. The identifications of Jesus which are offered first by the crowds and then by Peter are not rejected, but neither are they commended unequivocally. By putting the question of his identity directly to his disciples after he has been told of his reputation among the public, Jesus implicitly urges his followers to offer another identification of him. "Messiah" is perhaps more warmly accepted by Jesus, but only in an expressly limited way. The "son of man" usage puts its finger on the limitation, in that Jesus refers to his future suffering and vindication by means of the phrase, and it is precisely this that Peter objects to. Progressively, one approaches closer and closer to Jesus' own view of his identity in the passage, and the experiential use of biblical categories is developed in a critical way so that the distinctive elements of Jesus' mission are highlighted. The critical aspect of an approach to scripture is evident here, and it parallels Jesus' treatment of Targumic interpretation. The importance of this critical attitude is fundamental to the Caesarea Philippi passage; the early tradents of the Jesus story seem to have had his style of using Old Testament language and imagery ingrained in their material. For them, as for Jesus, scripture referred to the God who acted in the present, but it did not restrict God to a repetition of past acts. The critical style of interpretation permitted the past to be past, the present to be present, and, most crucially, God to be God.

In the Caesarea Philippi episode, the pattern of the experiential and critical use of scripture is manifest, but — as we have seen — the category "the son of man," although possessed of clearly biblical antecedents, receives a new point of reference. Matthew's version makes this especially clear, since he has Jesus ask, "Who do men say the son of man is?" (16:13). Basically, Jesus is here the content of the phrase. The interpretative style at this point becomes more than a

matter of using the Bible experientially or critically. The
case of the baptismal voice is similar. As we saw in part two,
the phrase "I am well pleased" appears in the Targum (41:8,
9; 42:1; 43:10) with a range of associations which helps to
explain its appearance in the words of the *bath qol*. In the
baptismal voice, however, the phrase is used of Jesus as
God's "son." The last term also has a rich background in the
Old Testament, appearing nearly five thousand times. It
expresses not only physical descent, but also such relationships as that between pupil and master (as, for example, in
the book of Proverbs). The usage "God's son" — or an
equivalent — is generally applied in the Old Testament to
speak of an intimate, but non-physical, relation between
God and the figure designated as "son"; to mention a few
prominent instances, it refers to angels (Genesis 6:2), God's
people as a whole (Exodus 4:22), the king in David's line (2
Samuel 7:14, cf. also Psalm 2:7), a supremely righteous man
(Wisdom 2:18). These applications help us to gather the
sense of the baptismal voice, but — especially as connected
to the phrase "I am well pleased," and its associations with a
figure who is addressed directly (Targum Isaiah 41:8, 9),
spoken of in connection with the spirit (Targum Isaiah
42:1), and identified as messiah (Targum Isaiah 43:10) —
"my son" in the *bath qol* cannot be limited in reference to
any one of these Old Testament usages, nor can it be understood as a simple combination of any group of them. In
short, the Caesarea Philippi sequence again evidences a
style of approach to biblical tradition which is similar to
that manifest in Jesus' use of Targumic interpretation. Now,
however, it has become clear that this style is not compre-
hended by calling it "experiential" and/or "critical"; there is
another aspect of it which needs to be described.

The parable of the vineyard (Matthew 21:33-36; Mark
12:1-12; Luke 20:9-19) relates to Targum Isaiah 5:1-7 in a
way which also reveals the aspect of Jesus' style of preaching
which we have yet to describe. In its specific application to
Israel's leaders, a connection between the parable and the
Targum seems evident, but the parable's narrative sequence
goes far beyond the imagery of the vineyard passage from

Isaiah. To some extent, of course, we do describe Jesus' development of Targumic imagery by calling it experiential and critical: he applies his tradition to his own experience, and in doing so he distances himself somewhat from his tradition. But to speak of Jesus as distancing himself from the biblical interpretation of his day, is to describe his style rather negatively. Can we find some description which will do justice to the new content which this style gives to old imagery (be it the vineyard, "the son of man," "my son" or God was "well pleased")?

Luke places a scene in which Jesus cites a passage from Isaiah at the beginning of Jesus' ministry (4:16-21). For Luke, this is the inauguration of Jesus' preaching, and v. 43 seems to indicate that he associated the message of the citation very closely with Jesus' programmatic preaching of the kingdom. Moreover, Luke seems to have foreshadowed Christian preaching in Diaspora synagogues by means of this scene (cf., for example, Acts 13:13-42), so that it becomes a model of missionary activity within his two volume work (cf. Chilton [1979] pp. 124-156 and [1981]). Luke essentially presents Jesus' citation in the wording of the Septuagint, as we might expect of this hellenistic Evangelist, and the synagogue procedure he speaks of may reflect the practice in the Diaspora more than that of Palestine in the time of Jesus. Nonetheless, the importance he gives to the scene might encourage us to investigate the style of the citation itself as an example of the preaching style of Jesus.

In Luke 4:18-19, Jesus applies an Old Testament passage to himself. Principally, he cites Isaiah 61:1-2a, and thereby identifies himself with the prophet who announced vindication and restoration to Israel on God's behalf. This association with the prophetic figure would be even more evident to Jesus' hearers if they had the interpretation of the Isaiah Targum in mind, because it introduces the passage with the characteristic phrase, "The prophet said." Jesus' experiential use of the passage is obvious, and is again tempered by a critical distancing from any known version of Isaiah 61. Jesus simply omits the phrase "to bind the broken in heart" from the text of Isaiah 61, and wording similar to Isaiah

58:6, a reference to setting the oppressed at liberty, has been inserted. Luke quite evidently was not responsible for these changes. He brought the traditional wording into line with that of the Septuagint, as is his habit (cf. Chilton [1979] pp. 157-177 and [1981] for suggestions as to the precise tradition before Luke), and would not likely have wished to omit one phrase and intercalate another. Moreover, the Septuagintal equivalent of the omitted phrase actually refers to healing, and would have suited the Lukan context very well (cf. vv. 22-30).

On the other hand, this change corresponds well to the style of Jesus' preaching as we have so far described it. The refinement appears to be part and parcel of a critical distancing away from certain language which appears in Isaiah. The message of the prophet is not only of divine favour (61:2a), but also of vengeance (v. 2b) against Gentiles (cf. v. 5). Jesus avoids the latter aspect, and later in the Lukan passage is portrayed as referring to incidents from the careers of Elijah and Elisha (4:25-27) by way of precedent for the conviction that the true prophet, unacceptable in his own land (v. 24), is sent precisely to the outcast. National vindication does not appear to be the burden of Jesus' message in the present instance, and the omission of the phrase "to bind the broken in heart" is understandable on this basis. The phrase in Isaiah is specifically applied to "the mourners in Zion" of v. 3, who are promised, not only simple restoration (vv. 3, 4), but also wealth at the expense of other nations (vv. 5, 6). Jesus uses the Isaian passage to speak of the poor, prisoners, the blind and the oppressed: the acceptable (δεκτόν) year of the Lord (v. 19) is promised to them, and for this reason Jesus is a prophet who is not acceptable (δεκτός) in his own country (v. 24). Luke's focus on the socially debilitated is famous (cf. H. Degenhardt [1965]), and even the rich in this Gospel must accept this emphasis in order to enjoy inclusion in Jesus' circle (cf. 14:12-14 and 19:1-10). But it would be wrong to claim that the motif as a whole is a Lukan invention, for the simple reason that it comes clearly to expression in Matthew and Mark, as well (cf., for example, Matthew 19:16-30; Mark

10:17-31, with Luke 18:18-30). The alteration in the Isaian passage, therefore, corresponds well both to Jesus' characteristic theology and to his style of preaching; for these reasons, it should be accepted at least as a good example of his interpretative approach to the Old Testament, and can be defended as an accurate representation of his message.

The importance of this passage from our point of view lies in the fact that it presents a longer citation from the book of Isaiah than is usual in Jesus' preaching. The two characteristics, experiential and critical, are already plain in what we have seen; Jesus uses the text to announce the present activity of God, whose acceptable year he says he proclaims, and at the same time alters the wording of the text in what is, on reflection, a crucial matter. But there is an obvious new content in what Jesus has to say, and this encourages us to ask, how does Jesus move from the Old Testament to the "text" he preaches? It is fashionable still to refer to Jesus' procedure as typological (cf. France [1971] pp. 38f. and G. W. H. Lampe and K. Woolcombe [1957]). A "type" (τύπος), in the understanding of the Church Fathers, was an Old Testament figure which was historical, but which only partially attests what is more fully revealed in the New Testament. For example, Isaac — on the point of being sacrificed on Mount Moriah (Genesis 22:1-14) — was from the second century viewed as a type of Christ on the way to the cross; Isaac prefigured the suffering obedience which was to find its complete expression in the crucifixion of Jesus.

Without question, typology is at least superior to allegory as a description of early Christian interpretation. On one occasion, Paul uses the language of allegory (Galatians 4:21-31, cf. especially v. 24) in order to apply the figures of Hagar and her son Ishmael to the covenant of Sinai and the present Jerusalem, and of Sarah and her son Isaac to his own view of covenant and the heavenly Jerusalem. Even here, however, Paul does not assert that the true meaning of Hagar and Sarah in symbolizing the two covenants is such that it takes over completely from their meaning within the Old Testament. As we have seen, Paul can view Isaac in another way, as representing Jesus, within the same letter, and his conviction that Abraham and those associated with him were the actual forebearers of Israel is foundational to his theological position as a whole. The term "allegory" is generally reserved for stories which are entirely figurative; that is, the elements in it serve only to refer to certain —usually specified — meanings, and have no value in themselves. Paul's procedure is really typological rather than allegorical in this case, and when — in a similar vein — he compares the exodus to the situation of the Corinthian community (1 Corinthians 10:1-13) he actually uses the language of types (cf. vv. 6, 11). For him the exodus was a real event, but its full significance could only be known in the light of Christ. When we call something in the Old Testament a type, we mean that it indicates the direction of a journey (be it to Moriah or the promised land) which is thought of as accomplished in the Jesus story.

In the present instance, however, it would appear strange to say that Jesus' use of the Old Testament is typological. Although Jesus does use the passage experientially, his critical application of it represents a marked departure from the perspective on salvation accepted in Isaiah 61: it is not merely a question of completing or intensifying what is said in the Old Testament, but of saying something new by means of the Old Testament text. For this reason, we can say only that Jesus' use of the passage is better understood as analogy than as typology. In saying that Isaiah 61:1, 2a is analogous to Luke 4:18, 19, we imply that there is a close relationship of wording between them, but we allow for the qualifications and the signal addition which Jesus contributed. By refusing to speak of typology in this context, we avoid giving the impression that Jesus wished to present his ministry merely as an extension of Isaiah's. In calling Jesus' style of interpretation analogical, we allow of the fresh convictions he brought to expression in referring to biblical tradition, and at the same time admit that the relationship between the text cited and the view of God he wishes to convey is very close. In effect, our use of the term "analogy" to characterize the relation between Jesus' use of biblical

tradition and that tradition itself is no more than a further
statement of the finding that Jesus used the contemporary
interpretation of the Bible experientially and critically. The
term does not develop our treatment any further, although
at least it does offer an alternative to characterizing Jesus'
use of the Old Testament as typological. Its principal advantage is that it refers to the positive new content which Jesus
brought to expression by using the Bible of his day.

In v. 21 of Luke 4, Jesus himself is portrayed as closing his
"reading" with the statement, "Today this scripture is fulfilled in your ears." The verb "fulfill" seems to have been
characteristic of Jesus' message: we find it in such important
contexts as his announcement of the kingdom (Mark 1:15)
and his explanation of the last meal with his disciples (Luke
22:16). In an article which appeared in 1968, Prof. Moule
shows that the term is basically used to speak of completion,
and this is to be distinguished from Matthew's use of the
verb to imply that the individual elements in a given Old
Testament passage actually appear in the Jesus story (cf.
Lindars [1961] p. 198). "Fulfilment" in the sense of completion would not be spoken of by Jesus, as we have observed,
in order to claim that Isaiah furnished an exact model for his
ministry, or a precise prophetic itinerary. His signal alteration of the expected text from Isaiah would appear to rule
such a supposition out. As altered, however, the "text"
described what Jesus intended to do in the synagogue: he
was sent, he claimed, to announce divine favour to those
who thought they had no chance to aspire to it. Similarly,
his parable of the vineyard — precisely in its departure from
the Isaian image in its Targumic presentation — addresses
divine judgment to his opponents in an unexpected way. In
both cases, Jesus can be understood as fulfilling or completing Isaiah, so long as we keep firmly in mind that he is not
simply implementing the programme (or "type") which he
found in that book or its Targum. Rather, Jesus completes
or fulfills what is lacking in the text itself by the introduction
of his own insight; he alters the text so that it becomes a
reflection of his experience of God.

The altered text is, in turn, handed on by Jesus, and later

by his followers, so that the same experience is available to others. The scripture is "fulfilled" in the sense that it mediates a fresh perception of God. The fulfilment style of Jesus stands out in the context of Jewish exegesis, but it also—and quite obviously—belongs to that context. The general tendency of Jewish interpretation of the Old Testament was to make the text apply to the contemporary situation in Israel. Midrash is perhaps the best known example; in this genre the opinions of various rabbis were systematically arranged according to the passages in a biblical book, set out in sequence. The end product was a compendious commentary containing all manner of dicta more or less relevant to the text cited. The Pesher, a genre of which representatives were found at Qumran, is at once more compact and more narrow in purpose. In the famous Habakkuk Pesher, the biblical book is related step by step to events in the past life of the community. Targum is the third and last form of rabbinic biblical interpretation, and refers to paraphrases of biblical books in Aramaic such as we have seen. Each of the genres could be said broadly to engage in the sort of interpretation applied by Jesus, since in all a pressing concern is to contemporize the text, to see its relevance to, respectively, rabbinic opinions, the development of the Qumran community and its ethos, and the popular understanding of the Bible in synagogue. So, as Jesus speaks of fulfilment "today," the Midrashim refer biblical texts to legal decisions which were still pertinent at the time of writing, the Pesherim present them as oracles, and the Targums consistently update their language to take account of contemporary conditions.

It is therefore not surprising that each genre has been hailed in recent years as the key to the New Testament's use of the Old Testament. One thinks in turn of Michael Goulder (1974, in respect of Midrash), Barnabas Lindars (1961, in respect of Pesher) and Martin McNamara (1972, in respect of Targum). While elements of each genre are unquestionably discernible in the New Testament, there are substantive differences in approach and purpose between Jesus and other Jewish interpreters. First, and most obviously, neither Jesus nor his followers was concerned to produce an extended exposition of the order of midrash, pesher or targum. In its own way, each of the latter three serves as a commentary on a book of scripture. But Jesus seems to have broken new ground, not in contemporizing scripture (which most intelligent preachers do), but in making God's present activity, not the text, his point of departure. The wealth and variety of biblical language and imagery in Jesus' sayings indicate that he did not use the circumstances of the present to explain the meaning of scripture; he rather used the scripture to assert God's meaning for the present. In Luke 4, the reaction of the synagogue congregation to Jesus' "reading" may well reflect some contemporary response to the innovative style of his preaching. In midrash, pesher and targum, the present is related to the text, which is the organizing principle of the whole enterprise; the fulfilment style also refers to the present, but here the present belongs immediately to God, and God's action, not the text, is the principal concern. To put the case a bit paradoxically, God's activity is the "text," and scripture is only the vehicle of expressing the present reality of God. That is the essentially distinctive element in Jesus' interpretation, and on this basis we can see why the fruit of a Hillel's exegesis is seen in various forms of commentaries, while the fruit of Jesus' preaching is the pluriform gospel of the kingdom.

Perhaps the dilemma in interpreting scripture today is that we use methods much like Hillel's and expect results akin to those achieved by Jesus. Rabbinic thinking was focused on the meaning of the biblical text and its application to contemporary circumstances. The presupposition of that focus, of course, was that the Bible was God's revelation, but in practice the rabbis' task was basically an interpretative one. Theological ideas were certainly involved in such interpretation, and they could be more determinative of contemporary belief and practice than any particular text, but the basic programme of the rabbis was oriented towards scripture. Jesus' orientation was somewhat different, and this fact corresponds to his role as a popular teacher rather than a professional academic. He used scripture as a starting point in his preaching, and therefore as a vehicle of his vision of God, but understanding scripture was not for him the goal of preaching. His task, as he understood it, was not essentially interpretative. It is therefore hardly surprising that we in the Church are today concerned with the question of hermeneutics. The style of Jesus was a matter of using texts, not simply interpreting them, and of fulfilling them with a fresh statement of the activity of God. From the beginning, we must acknowledge that no account of the use of the Bible can be held to be consistent with the preaching of Jesus which stops with the mere question of what a text means.

Similarly, a historical critical approach to the Bible is proper — and necessary — to our intellectual quest for its meaning, but the significance of the Bible as preached by Jesus is not simply a function of its historical or intellectual value. Criticism (in the basic sense of the word) was certainly involved in what Jesus was doing, but his programme was not limited to that. His style involved asserting God's rule by means of using scripture. The historian can, and ought to, perceive this, but as a historian he cannot put the programme into practice. Practising the style of Jesus is a matter of faith, and for this reason an unbending adherence to a historical approach can be an inhibition in the experience of believers and preachers. After one has grasped a text historically as fully as possible, its intended meaning may be reasonably clear, but its significance as an articulation of faith can only be expressed if the reader uses the text as an occasion for reflecting on his own experience of God. Our difficulty in this regard makes our reconstruction of Jesus' style of preaching important within contemporary discussion.

There is the possibility that we can use the Bible — Old Testament and New — within the fulfilment style of Jesus. We can approximate this style by working back through its three characteristics as we have come to know them: analogical, critical, experiential. By allowing that a biblical passage might present an analogy to our present circumstances, we take the first step towards a fulfilled interpretation. The story of Abraham's willingness to sacrifice Isaac in Genesis 22 has already been mentioned. The story may be greeted with shock, since God's demand for the beloved son seems terribly ruthless. But suppose the reader were to accept what happened to Abraham as analogous with his own position. Can he think of no corner of his life in which God has demanded self-denial? Naturally he can, but this is not to say that his experience is the direct equivalent of Abraham's. By dealing with the passage as an analogy, he can reflect on the extent to which it accords with his situation and on the ways in which it is different. Such critical meditation enables us to see how God addresses us through the text, because we are able to specify those aspects of the passage which are not pertinent to our experience. In this manner, we are led to a critical identification with Abraham: he becomes the paradigm for our faith because it is faith and faith alone that we share with him. As we read about Abraham's relationship with God, our own is brought to mind, and so the text awakens and describes our own experience in faith. At that moment — when interpertation is analogical, critical and experiential — we imitate the fulfilled style pioneered by Jesus.

Our imitation brings us to the point where our faith is awakened, but we are not yet addressed by God. Yet it is the central purpose of Jesus' style of interpretation to articulate what God is saying, not just our belief in him. Jesus did not rest content in calling men to faith in God; his whole burden was to express and enact the purposes of God themselves. For this reason, our style of interpretation is only fulfilled in the way that Jesus' was when we move beyond an experience of our own faith to an experience of God. At that moment, and not before, God addresses us through the text. He makes demands through Genesis 22, manifestly unreasonable demands, which he expects us to meet. He commands what is most dear to us in his service: perhaps time, energy, abilities, ambitions are all to be shaped to his glory. Family, friends and leisure may have to take second place; in some cases a sacrifice is required, and there is no angel to explain it is only a test. Then again, perhaps it is the reader's understanding of his own vocation which God wishes to be given up, and he is not happy with a purposive introspection which feels secure in itself. When all this and more comes to mind, when scripture awakens in us a sense of God to which we are expectantly and fearfully attentive, our interpretation is fulfilled, and we are in a position to believe and to preach. As we permit ourselves to stand under God's word to us in this way, he speaks also in a softer, more encouraging voice. Just as we consider how much is required of those who follow the example of Abraham, we recall that Paul compared what Abraham was willing to do on Moriah to what God actually did on Golgotha: "He did not spare his own son" (Romans 8:32, a quotation of Genesis 22:16). God demands so much precisely because he has given — and continues to give — everything. He has withheld nothing, and with careless grace has opened the way of selfless service. He desires us to become what he is, and he is ruthless in pursuit of this fulfilment.

The fact that Paul refers to Genesis 22 in Romans invites us to return to the question of the relationship between the Testaments in light of what we have said about the fulfilment style of Jesus. Can the New Testament be said in this case to fulfill the Old Testament? The answer to that question must be "no," if by "fulfill" one implies that a prediction is accomplished, or even that a type or programme is achieved. The story about Abraham and Isaac on Moriah and the passion of Golgotha each maintains its distinctive value, even though the other may help us to see it in a fresh way. Paul, as we have seen repeatedly, by no means believed that Abraham and his activities were merely symbols for what was to come. But in Romans 8:32 Paul may be said to be practising the fulfilment style of Jesus' preaching. The analogy of Abraham is there used to explain God's love, and the analogy depends on the reader's awareness of the critical difference between God and Abraham: God actually gave what Abraham was in the end permitted to keep. If the reader is aware of this distinction, he may share Paul's experience of God as a father pressed to make the ultimate sacrifice. This sort of fulfilment is not at all of the nature of supercession. Romans 8:32 does not replace Genesis 22; indeed, you will never understand the former without the latter. The same may be said of the use Jesus made of the Isaiah Targum. The fulfilment style does not remove, but confirms, the value of the Old Testament as Jesus' scripture. At the same time, it opens the possibility of using scripture, as Jesus did, in order to discover, express and propagate our distinctive experience of God in the present.

Once "fulfilment" is defined with reference to the preaching style of Jesus, one cannot be content with saying, "The Old Testament is fulfilled in the New Testament." Rather, one sees that Jesus and his followers saw their Bible (roughly speaking, what we call the Old Testament) as fulfilled, and this prompts the question, "In my experience, do I see my Bible (of two Testaments) fulfilled?" By definition, "fulfilment" describes a fresh mediation of God through the biblical text. Yesterday's fulfilment is for the historian; today's is for the believer. The claim of a speaker or writer in the New Testament that the Old Testament is fulfilled in a given event is a matter for simple historical observation. But the reflection on whether that fulfilment corresponds in some way to the activity of God in the present is of a different order. Moreover, the fulfilment style of Jesus is not such as to suggest that only those Old Testament passages which happen to be cited in the New Testament may be relevant to our faith experience. Rather, his preaching style is an invitation to collate and express our experience of God with scripture.

The distinctive element, or at least a distinctive element, in the New Testament is precisely the preaching style of Jesus. The style directs us back to the Old Testament as scripture; there can be no question of reducing the Old Testament to a preamble to the "real Bible" on the basis of Jesus' position. The richness of experience reflected in the Old Testament, a richness which supercedes that of the New

Testament in its variety and in the scale of time it involves, makes it for Jesus and his followers an indispensable thesaurus for describing what God is doing. The authority of the Old Testament resides in its usefulness in such descriptions, and the New Testament can be applied in a similar way. As I have already suggested, however, the New Testament cannot compare with the Old Testament in the richness of experience reflected, and for this reason it is less useful as a thesaurus of God's activity. The New Testament makes its particular contribution, not in its addition of new experiences, but in its guidance on how the biblical thesaurus as a whole is to be used. The vividness and drama of the New Testament should not be sold short, but most of the events and sayings we find in it have some sort of precedents in the Old Testament, even though such elements are presented in a thoroughly fresh way and may relate to radically new happenings. But the New Testament does, based on Jesus' preaching, give us something the Old Testament does not: a clear suggestion of how the Bible might be used within the context of faith.

The authority of the Bible is therefore only recognizable when the reader is mindful of his experience of God, as well as of the text before him. Its authority is not inherent in the written text as such. Our position in this regard corresponds somewhat to that of the people whom the Bible describes. James Barr has lucidly explained (1980, p. 117) that in most of the history of Israel and at the time of Jesus and his first followers, the whole of faith was not in any sense consigned to writing. Reference to written documents only occurs, Barr maintains, within the development of a given community of faith (p. 121, cf. pp. 54, 126). Our analysis of faith as a power which defines communities, and particularly our description of the trans-temporal community which is defined by a biblically based faith, is in substantive accord with Prof. Barr's views. Indeed, his programme of how the Bible should be used in our churches agrees at many points with my own suggestions (pp. 122, 123). But there is a significant sense in which the suggestions of the present volume differ from Barr's. Barr rightly sees that to speak of the Bible's "authority" is only meaningful within believing communities, but he considers that for such communities the Bible provides the binding or normative expression of how God is experienced. (The word he actually uses, in italics, is "classic" [p. 122].) In Barr's thinking, inspiration is constantly available from God, who cannot be less accessible to one age than he is to another, but inspiration also produced the Bible on a once for all basis as a paradigm of relationship with God. In his argument, from the time the canon was agreed, theology has been a matter of exegesis (p. 125, cf. pp. 63, 124). He is wisely concerned not to give the impression that the Bible, as such, should be the object of faith (p. 126), and he studiously avoids any suggestion that biblical standards of behaviour can be applied directly to today's ethical questions (pp. 130-133). But he must defend himself against these possible misunderstandings of his position precisely because he ascribes paradigmatic authority to the Bible; for him, biblical authority amounts to control of, not just influence on, believing communities.

This control, however, is in Barr's mind not exercised in the realm of ethics, nor even in that of the way that belief is formulated, but in the pictures of God the Bible conveys. He repeatedly states (cf. pp. 36, 46, 60, 126f.) that the Bible is a book for the future in the sense that it tells of how God will be. At first sight, this formulation would seem to ascribe an oracular authority to the Bible, and in fact Barr admits (p. 115) that, read at face value in the context of faith, the Bible looks rather as fundamentalists have said it does. It is for this reason that Barr believes historical criticism is crucial; the book of oracles would have to be said to consist of *inerrant* oracles, except that modern historical study saves us from making this palpably misleading statement. Historical criticism alone permits us to see the Bible as a collection of faith-statements by people in the past (p. 115), so that it is really to these people that we are directed in the quest for a paradigm of faith (p. 47, cf. pp. 48, 60, 113f.). At just this point, Barr seems to be overtaken by a fallacy which also afflicts Dennis Nineham's position. As we have seen, Prof. Nineham looks to the origins of the Christian community for the attestation of saving events which provide the basis of faith. At times, indeed, Nineham would appear to argue that historical inquiry generally can take the place of theological evaluation (1977, pp. 160-165). Barr, it must be said, far more scrupulously draws the necessary distinction between history and theology (1980, pp. 26, 28, 45, 124). Yet for Barr the subject matter of theology is essentially biblical, so that he can even make the for him unguarded comment that what he calls "salvation" belongs to the people and events in the Bible (p. 47). A certain version of the inspiration of history has — as in the case of Nineham — taken the place of the inspiration of the biblical text.

The route taken by Barr to faith through history is rather similar to Nineham's, and in both the ascription of a sacred status to biblical history is taken for granted. In this context, it is notable that neither Barr (p. 16) nor Nineham (pp. 65-66) feels it is important to raise and discuss critically the question of God's existence and activity: they both simply proceed on the assumption that the Bible (or rather, the history behind the Bible) provides the correct presupposition on this point. Historically, as we have seen, one cannot justify such assumptions. Theologically, it seems easier and more economical to raise the question of God directly rather than to resuscitate a salvation historical scheme by appealing to the paradigmatic authority of people from the past. But even putting these considerations aside, we have seen that an appreciation of Jesus' fulfilment style of preaching is not consistent with a view of revelation according to which the past is somehow more holy than the present. Jesus did not for a moment, of course, deny even implicitly that his Bible presented pictures of God as active, nor did he fail to see the relevance of those pictures for his own time. But he does not seem to have limited himself to the biblical text in order to describe the contemporary activity of God. Sometimes, indeed, he deviated from the Bible signally, and with some critical acumen. As long as we see the Bible as the manual of how we must see God, instead of as the book of how we might see him, its authority as fulfiled by Jesus will continue to elude us. No hermeneutical theory, no matter

how complicated, can approximate Jesus' style of preaching
unless it takes account of the individual's apprehension of
God, nor can our trust in the faith of Israel or of the early
Church replace our own trust in God.

Our appeal for the necessity of giving play to the individual's apprehension of God may well seem threatening to
many Christians. Some will see it as a diminution of the
Bible's authority, while others will complain it gives too
much scope to personal visions of (or delusions about) God.
To these understandable objections, some reply should be
offered. First, I would stress that our picture of the present
interpretative position is based on a historical reconstruction of Jesus' style of preaching and on ordinary critical
reflection. One may or may not wish the case to be otherwise, but unless I have made a series of dreadful errors,
Jesus claimed to speak of God directly by means of biblical
language and imagery as they were understood in his time,
and he taught his followers to practise a similar directness in
speaking of God as he actually is. Within this style of belief
and preaching, the Bible is a means rather than an end. To
those who see religion essentially as a matter of venerating
tradition, be it exegetical, liturgical or hierarchical tradition, Jesus' teaching will always seem dangerously subjective. Similarly, I might be wrong in my rejection of the
options presented by fundamentalist and salvation historical approaches to the Bible, but I do not see that there are
evidential or critical issues which I have seriously misrepre-
sented in my analysis of the present interpretative position.
If the case is as I see it, then our views on biblical authority
and the individual's importance will simply have to change.
Secondly, however, I would strongly maintain that the
Bible's authority as here presented can be defended ration-
ally and taught honestly. "When I read the Bible, I am
presented with God as I know him": such a formulation
seems to me consistent with Jesus' style of preaching. It is
perhaps less grandiose than saying the Bible is inerrant, or
paradigmatic, or the like, but it is truer to the way Jesus used
the Old Testament as it was understood in his day.

The present formulation also shifts the discussion about

biblical authority away from complex vocabulary and towards a simple issue: when you read the Bible, do you encounter God, or not? In fundamentalist circles, the word "inerrant" has been subject to some rather contorted personal definitions in the attempt to apply it to the Bible accurately. I once heard "inerrant" defined by a noted conservative scholar to refer to that which would not lead astray the earnest seeker after truth, a description which I hope would apply to most of the things I read. Such private definitions remind us that there is no such thing as objective recourse to any tradition, no matter how perfect it may be thought to be. In order to be believed, tradition must be interpreted and appropriated by individuals.

Appeals to biblical inerrancy and salvation history attempt on occasion to short circuit the rightful place of the individual by claiming the tradition carries a true interpretation implicit in it, namely inerrancy and historical revelation. Both of these interpretations, however, are nothing other than evaluations of the significance of the Bible, and not part of the message of the Bible. As evaluations, of course, they are harmless, and they can be positively valuable as representations of what an individual comes to believe as he reads the biblical text. They are accounts of the significance of the Bible which anyone might use, tentatively or with enthusiasm, in order to express what he thinks the text means in his experience, if only provisionally. But when they are taken up as the party lines of fundamentalist and liberal Christianity, individuals are coerced by social pressure to accept them, not merely as hypotheses or presuppositions, but as orthodox teaching.

The party line in practice has as much importance as the biblical text, and among such groups ignorance about the Bible suggests that careful reading is not valued as much as one might think it reasonably would be. Indeed, insofar as the individual is convinced that his adherence to the party line is crucial, he is likely not to express, or even admit, he has formed an impression from the biblical text which seems to contradict what he has been taught to expect. Change is then only possible as a consensus revision of the tradition as a whole in which it is claimed that the new dogma was always somehow implicit or intended in the party line. Groups generally styled as fundamentalist have most often been liable to descriptions of this kind, largely because their party lines are formally stated. (When they are so stated, and individuals are required to submit to such formulations as to creeds, I am inclined to use the word with a capital "F.") But liberal Christianity has its own shibboleths, such as "myth," "salvation history" and "Christ-event." A refusal to accept certain views about such terms will preclude admission to some circles, and the mechanism of exclusion (be it formal or not) attests the force which certain dogmas exercise in the minds of group members generally.

Belief is a matter of cognition. When one perceives a situation, however specific or complex, one acts in a certain way, or decides to do nothing, on the strength of his perception. The perception called faith is necessarily subjective, in that only individuals as cognitive subjects are capable of believing, trusting, and undertaking the consequent moral action. Fundamentalist and liberal attempts to obviate this necessary subjectivity only lead to unfruitful exercises in private definition and revisionism. All such attempts confuse individual faith in God with group assent to a doctrine. Indeed, the extent to which fundamentalists and liberals are willing to pass over the entire question of God with the bland observation that the Bible assumes he exists suggests that their dogmatism is not theologically fruitful.

Faith is individual and subjective, even though it belongs to people living in communities, and endowed with the ability to communicate and articulate their faith insofar as they live in communities. Their attempt to correlate their beliefs, impressions, praise, convictions and anxieties with one another and with communities of faith from the past should not be mistaken for a confusion of faith itself with a given expression of faith. If God is the object, the only proper object, of my faith, then my belief must be as dynamic as he is. As Abraham on Moriah, I must be ready for and responsive to the unexpected, no matter how surprising it might be. This may involve denying what I know to be a biblical promise only in order to possess it again all the more securely, as in the case of Abraham, or the recognition that as a follower of Jesus the mere willingness to sacrifice oneself is not always enough. But no matter what the case may be, I will know that the faith I have is my faith, and not the ideological hand-me-down of my culture. On that basis, I can be of far more use to those around me, whether they assent to my beliefs or not.

Our remarks on Genesis 22 are, of course, only intended to be taken by way of example. They instance the way I imagine the fulfilment style of Jesus can be applied to the Bible, and indeed the way in which I personally have tried to apply it. As such, our example is not intended as any sort of manual for preachers, but only as an incentive for believing readers and preachers to use the fulfilment style of Jesus as we have come to understand it. His approach to the Bible is — within strictly historical terms — a prominent feature of his thought and ministry, and — within theological terms —of central importance for understanding what it is to believe, and to use scripture as a vehicle for belief. The fulfilment style of Jesus challenges those of us who confess a biblical faith to identify our experience of God by means of the Bible, and not to rest content with venerating the book itself. For the rest of us, his style offers an important instance of belief, one which we can hardly ignore in articulating our own. No matter which group one belongs to, Jesus' fulfilled interpretation points to a different sort of orientation in the world from those which are commonly available, and so may lead to a fresh appraisal of what it means to be alive, to think and to believe.

Appendix I

JESUS AND "THE SERVANT"

Preachers today still commonly identify Jesus with the figure called God's servant in the book of Isaiah; "the suffering servant" (as the figure has been named in modern criticism) is said to endure affliction, die and be vindicated (cf. 52:13—53:12). There does seem to be an allusion to this passage in 1 Peter 2:22-25; the story of Jesus triggered a reminiscence of scripture in the mind of the writer. (Indeed, the relationship here between the scripture and the Jesus story reminds us of the fulfilment style of preaching we have described in the conclusion.) But there is a world of difference between seeing such allusions and claiming that Jesus himself claimed to be the servant spoken of by Isaiah. Morna Hooker has shown that these quotations do not imply that Jesus fulfills the role of "the suffering servant" ([1959] p. 149). On only one occasion does Jesus himself cite a "servant" passage (Luke 22:37) according to the Gospels, and in that instance it is his being reckoned with transgressors, not his suffering, that he draws attention to. The evidence is simply too slender to support the contention that Jesus or even his followers saw the servant spoken of in Isaiah as a detailed model of his ministry.

The fact remains, however, that "servant" passages are associated with Jesus in the New Testament, and the term "servant" itself is a prominent designation of Jesus, especially in the narratives of his baptism. Prof. Hooker is no doubt correct to argue that the use of the word "servant" and a few citations from Isaiah do not substantiate the claim that a figure predicted by Isaiah was actualized by Jesus in the teaching of the New Testament. On the other hand, the question remains: why was such language used at all? A consideration of the Isaiah Targum suggests there is a straightforward answer to our question. The Targum shows us that the term "servant" could be taken as a designation of the messiah (cf. 43:10). This is particularly the case at 52:13 and 53:10. The Targum indeed interprets 52:13—53:12 as a whole so as to insist on the glorification of the messiah, but it also — in an apparently early reading — refers to the possibility that the messiah might die (53:12 "he delivered his soul to death"). In other words, the Targum offers no support for anything like a "suffering servant" motif in early Judaism of which Jesus might have availed himself, but it does speak of a *messianic servant* commissioned by God whose ministry involves at least the risk of death (cf. Chilton [1982] pp. 86-96). That such language was applied to Jesus was a natural result of the conviction he was God's messiah and of knowledge of his death. The citation of the relevant passages in Isaiah by followers of Jesus who were familiar with Targumic tradition is quite explicable. That Jesus himself used such language as he faced death for claiming (explicitly or not) to be God's messiah is also a possibility which ought to be held open.

Appendix II

ADDITIONAL TARGUMIC PASSAGES

Certain other passages in the Isaiah Targum were investigated in the course of the present study. They did not present striking enough analogies with dominical logia to justify including them in the body of the book, and I would not say that the importance of the Targum to the student of Jesus' teaching is proved by them. Nonetheless, it would be unhelpful to those who might wish to pursue the line of inquiry developed here not to mention them briefly:

Targum Isaiah 14:12 (cf. Luke 10:18): the imagery of the Targum might just have influenced the picture of Satan's fall in the saying of Jesus (cf. Tárrech [1978]).

Targum Isaiah 33:11 (cf. Matthew 3:12/Luke 3:17): the statement in the Targum that God's "word" will destroy as whirlwind scatters chaff is reminiscent of the preaching of John the Baptist.

Targum Isaiah 34:12 (cf. John 8:33): the claim to be free sons is in the Targum a symptom of insolent pride, which is what Jesus is pictured as condemning in John.

Targum Isaiah 52:13 (cf. John 12:34): the exaltation of the messiah in the Targum might provide some of the background to the motif of the son being lifted up (cf. Chilton [1980[4]]).

Appendix III

"AMEN"

In a recent article (Chilton [1978²]), I pointed out that "amen" in the Greek New Testament might be the Hellenistic equivalent of the more primitive, Aramaic usage "in truth." On three occasions (37:18; 45:14, 15), "in truth" appears in the Isaiah Targum at the beginning of a sentence as a solemn asseveration. This provides an exact parallel to certain passages in the Old Syriac Gospels, written in a later dialect of Aramaic; these passages suggest that "in truth" was the Aramaic tradition which the Greek Gospel writers rendered as "amen," which is probably not a Semitic idiom (cf. Berger [1970]). The Isaiah Targum confirms that "in truth" was used by Aramaic speakers as an introductory asseveration, which is the usage in question in the sayings of Jesus. It also shows that, in using such a locution, Jesus would not have been entirely original; he was more probably echoing a convention, as was his habit, which his hearers were familiar with from regular worship in their synagogues.

BIBLIOGRAPHY

1. Primary Sources (convenient editions of works cited):

Aland, K., und Aland, B., *Novum Testamentum Graece.* Deutsche Bibelstiftung, 1979.

Aland, K., Black, M., Martini, C. M., Metzger, B. M., Wikgren, A., *The Greek New Testament.* Würtemberg Bible Society, 1968 (and 1975).

Blackman, P., *Mishnayoth.* Judaica, 1964.

Braude, W. G., *Pesikta Rabbati.* Yale University, 1968.

Charles, R. H., *The Apocrypha and Pseudepigrapha.* Clarendon, 1913 (and reprints).

Díez Macho, A., *Neophyti I.* Consejo Superior de Investigaciones Científicas, 1968-1979.

Epstein, I., *The Babylonian Talmud.* Soncino, 1935-1952.

Etheridge, J. W., *The Targums of Onkelos and Jonathan ben Uzziel.* Ktav, 1968 (from 1862-1865).

Freedman, H., and Simon, M., *Midrash Rabbah.* Soncino, 1939.

Guillaumont, A., Puech, H.-Ch., Quispel, G., Till, W., 'Abd al Masīh, Y., *The Gospel according to Thomas.* Brill, 1959 (and reprints).

Lauterbach, J. Z., *Mekilta de-Rabbi Ishmael.* Jewish Publication Society, 1933 (and reprints).

Petuchowski, J. J., "Jewish Prayer Texts of the Rabbinic Period" in: Petuchowski and Brocke, M., *The Lord's Prayer and Jewish Liturgy.* Seabury, 1978.

Sperber, A., *The Bible in Aramaic.* Brill, 1959-1973.

Stenning, J. F., *The Targum of Isaiah.* Clarendon, 1949.

Torrey, C. C., *The Lives of the Prophets.* Society of Biblical Literature, 1946.

2. Secondary Literature

Anderson, H., *The Gospel of Mark.* Oliphants, 1976.

Baker, D. L., *Two Testaments, One Bible.* Inter-Varsity, 1976.

Banks, R. J., *Jesus and the Law in the Synoptic Tradition.* Cambridge University, 1975.

Barnard, L. W., *Justin Martyr.* Cambridge University, 1967.

Barr, J., *Fundamentalism.* SCM, 1977.

_____, *The scope and authority of the Bible.* SCM, 1980.

Barth, K., *The Epistle to the Romans.* Oxford University, 1933 (and reprints).

Berger, K., *Die Amen-Worte Jesu.* Berlin, de Gruyter, 1970.

Billerbeck, P. and Strack, H. L., *Kommentar zum Neuen Testament aus Talmud und Midrasch.* München, Beck, 1924-1928 (and reprints): 1926 (Matthew), 1924 (Mark-Acts).

Black, M., *An Aramaic Approach to the Gospels and Acts.* Clarendon, 1967.

Bloch, M., *The Historian's Craft*. Manchester University, 1976 (a reprint).

Bornkam, G., "μνοτήριον, μνέω" in: Kittel, G., ed., *Theological Dictionary of the New Testament*. Eerdmans, 1967, from the German edition of 1942.

Bowker, J., "The Son of Man" (*Journal of Theological Studies*, 1977).

——————, *The Targums and Rabbinic Literature*. Cambridge University, 1969.

Bruce, F. F., *New Testament History*. Nelson, 1969 (and reprints).

Büchler, A., *Types of Jewish-Palestinian Piety*. Jews' College, 1922 (and a reprint).

Burton, E. D., *Syntax of the Moods and Tenses in New Testament Greek*. Clark, 1966 (from 1898).

Chilton, B. D., "'Amen' — an Approach through Syriac Gospels" (*Zeitschrift für die neutestamentliche Wissenschaft*, 1978²).

——————, "Announcement in *Nazara*" in: France, R. T., and Wenham, D., eds., *Gospel Perspectives* II. JSOT, 1981.

——————, "A Comparative Study of Synoptic Development" (*Journal of Biblical Literature*, 1982³).

——————, *The Glory of Israel: The Theology and Provenience of the Isaiah Targum*. JSOT, 1982.

——————, *God in Strength: Jesus' Announcement of the Kingdom*, Freistadt, Plöchl, 1979.

——————, "Isaac and the Second Night" (*Biblica*, 1980¹).

——————, "Jesus ben David" (*Journal for the Study of the New Testament*, 1982²).

——————, "John XII 34 and Targum Isaiah LII 13" (*Novum Testamentum*, 1980⁴).

_____, "Regnum Dei Deus Est" (*Scottish Journal of Theology,* 1978).

_____, "Targumic Transmission and Dominical Tradition" in: France, R. T., and Wenham, D., *Gospel Perspectives* I. JSOT, 1980².

_____, "The Transfiguration" (*New Testament Studies,* 1980³).

Churgin, P., *Targum Jonathan to the Prophets.* Yale University, 1927. (N.b., the date on the title page is incorrect.)

Cohn-Sherbok, D. M., "An Analysis of Jesus' Arguments Concerning the Plucking of Grain on the Sabbath" (*Journal for the Study of the New Testament,* 1979).

_____, "Jesus' Defence of the Resurrection of the Dead" (*Journal for the Study of the New Testament,* 1981).

Collins, J. J., *The Sibylline Oracles of Egyptian Judaism.* Society of Biblical Literature, 1974.

Dalman, G. H., *The Words of Jesus.* Clark, 1902.

Davies, P. R., and Chilton, B. D., "The Aqedah: A Revised Tradition History" (*Catholic Biblical Quarterly,* 1978).

Degenhardt, H. J., *Lukas: Evangelist der Armen.* Stuttgart, KBW, 1965.

de Jonge, M., "The Use of the Word 'Anointed' in the Time of Jesus" (*Novum Testamentum,* 1966).

Díez Macho, A., "Le Targum palestinien" in: Ménard, J.-E., ed., *Exégèse Biblique et Judaïsme.* Strasbourg, Faculté de Théologie catholique, 1973.

Eppstein, V., "The historicity of the Gospel account of the Cleansing of the Temple" (*Zeitschrift fur die neutestamentliche Wissenschaft,* 1964).

Farmer, W. R., *The Synoptic Problem.* Collier-Macmillan, 1964 and Dillsboro, Western North Carolina, 1976.

Fitzmyer, J. A., *The Genesis Apocryphon of Qumran Cave 1*. Pontifical Biblical Institute, 1966 and 1971.

————, "The Languages of Palestine in the First Century A.D." (*Catholic Biblical Quarterly*, 1970).

————, *A Wandering Aramaean*. Scholars, 1979.

France, R. T., *Jesus and the Old Testament*. Tyndale, 1971.

Frankel, Z., *Zu dem Targum der Propheten*. Breslau, Schletter, 1872.

Freed, E. D., *Old Testament Quotations in the Gospel of John*. Brill, 1965.

Gardner-Smith, P., *Saint John and the Synoptic Gospels*. Cambridge University, 1938.

Gerhardsson, B., *The Origins of the Gospel Traditions*. SCM, 1979.

Ginzberg, L., *An Unknown Jewish Sect*. Jewish Theological Seminary, 1976.

Goldberg, A. M., *Untersuchungen über die Vorstellung von der Schekhinah*. Berlin, de Gruyter, 1969.

Goulder, M. D., *The Evangelists' Calendar*. SPCK, 1978.

————, *Midrash and Lection in Matthew*. SPCK, 1974.

Grant, R. M., *A Short History of the Interpretation of the Bible*. Collier-Macmillan, 1972. Earlier versions appeared in 1948, 1963, 1965.

Gray, G. B., *A Critical and Exegetical Commentary on the Book of Isaiah*. Clark, 1912 (and reprints).

Grelot, P., "Deux tosephtas targumiques inédites sur Isaïe LXVI" (*Revue Biblique*, 1972).

————, "A propos d'une tosephta targumique" (*Revue Biblique*, 1973).

Griñó, R., "El Meturgeman y Neofiti I" (*Biblica*, 1977).

Grundmann, W., *Das Evangelium nach Lukas*. Berlin, Evangelische Verlagsanstalt, 1969.

_____, *Das Evangelium nach Markus*. Berlin, Evangelische Verlagsanstalt, 1959.

_____, *Das Evangelium nach Matthaus*. Berlin, Evangelische Verlagsanstalt, 1971.

Gundry, R. H., *The Use of the Old Testament in St. Matthew's Gospel*. Brill, 1967.

Gunn, D. M., *King David*. JSOT, 1978.

Hanson, A. T., *Jesus Christ in the Old Testament*. SPCK, 1965.

Hengel, M., *The Son of God*. SCM, 1976.

Hertz, J. H., "Foreword" in: Epstein, I., ed., *The Babylonian Talmud: Seder Nezikin* I. Soncino, 1935.

Hill, D., *The Gospel of Matthew*. Oliphants, 1972.

Holtz, T., *Untersuchungen über die alttestamentlichen Zitate bei Lukas*. Akademie, 1968.

Hooker, M. D., *Jesus and the Servant*. SPCK, 1959.

Jeremias, J., "γέεννα" in: Kittel, G., ed., *Theological Dictionary of the New Testament*. Eerdmans, 1964, from the German edition of 1933.

_____, "παῖς Θεοῦ . . . D. παῖς Θεοῦ in the New Testament" in: Kittel, G., ed., *Theological Dictionary of the New Testament*. Eerdmans, 1967, from the German edition of 1954.

_____, *The Parables of Jesus*. SCM, 1972, with previous and subsequent English and German editions.

Johnson, S. E., "The Biblical Quotations in Matthew" (*Harvard Theological Review*, 1943).

Kähler, K. M. A., *Der sogenannte historische Jesus und der geschichtliche, biblische Christus.* Leipzig, Deichert, 1896 (cf. the English edition, Fortress, 1964).

Kaufman, S. A., "The Job Targum from Qumran" (*Journal of the American Oriental Society*, 1973).

Kimelman, R., "Birkat Ha-Minim and the Lack of Evidence for an Anti-Christian Jewish Prayer in Late Antiquity" in Sanders, E.P., ed., *Jewish and Christian Self-Definition* II. SCM, 1981.

Kock, K., "Messias und Sündenvergebung in Jesaya 53 — Targum" (*Journal of Semitic Studies*, 1972).

Kosmala, H., "Matthew XXVI 52 — A Quotation from the Targum" (*Novum Testamentum*, 1960).

——————, "The Parable of the Unjust Steward in the Light of Qumran" (*Annual of the Swedish Theological Institute*, 1964).

Lagrange, M. J., *Evangile selon Saint Marc.* Gabalda, 1929 (and 1947).

——————, *Evangile selon Saint Matthieu.* Gabalda, 1927 (and reprints).

Lampe, G. W. H., and Woollcombe, K., *Essays on Typology.* SCM, 1957.

Lane, W. L., *The Gospel according to Mark.* Marshall, Morgan & Scott, 1974.

Lash, N., "What might martyrdom mean?" in: Horbury, W., and McNeil, B., eds., *Suffering and Martyrdom in the New Testament.* Cambridge University, 1981.

Lentzen-Deis, F., *Dei Taufe Jesu nach den Synoptikern.* Frankfort, Knecht, 1970.

Levey, S. H., "The Date of Targum Jonathan to the Prophets" (*Vetus Testamentum*, 1971).

Lindars, B., *New Testament Apologetic.* SCM, 1961.

Lonergan, B. F. J., *Method in Theology.* Herder, 1973.

McNamara, M., *The New Testament and the Palestinian Targum to the Pentateuch.* Pontifical Biblical Institute, 1966.

——————, *Targum and Testament.* Irish University, 1972.

McNeile, A. H., *The Gospel According to St. Matthew.* Macmillan, 1915.

Maier, G., *The End of the Historical-Critical Method.* Concordia, 1977. (from the German editions of 1974 and 1975).

Manson, T. W., *The Teaching of Jesus.* Cambridge University, 1955 (from the second edition of 1935).

Marshall, I. H., *The Gospel of Luke.* Paternoster, 1978.

Moore, G. F., *Judaism in the First Centuries of the Christian Era.* Harvard University, 1927[1] (volume 1), 1927[2] (volume 2).

Moule, C. F. D., "Fulfilment-words in the New Testament" (*New Testament Studies,* 1968).

——————, *The Origin of Christology.* Cambridge University, 1977.

——————, "'Through Jesus Christ our Lord': Some Questions about the Use of Scripture" (*Theology,* 1977).

Murphy-O'Connor, J., "A Literary Analysis of Damascus Document VI:2—VIII:3" (*Revue Biblique,* 1971).

Neusner, J., *A History of the Jews in Babylonia.* Brill, 1965 (volume 1), 1966 (volume 2).

——————, "'Judaism' after Moore: A Programmatic Statement" (*Journal of Jewish Studies,* 1980).

——————, *Judaism: The Evidence of the Mishnah.* Chicago University, 1982.

——————, *The Rabbinic Traditions about the Pharisees.* Brill, 1971.

Nineham, D. E., *Explorations in Theology.* SCM, 1977.

Perrin, N., *Jesus and the Language of the Kingdom.* SCM, 1976.

——————, *Rediscovering the Teaching of Jesus.* SCM, 1967.

Pesch, R., *Das Markusevangelium I. Teil.* Herder, 1976.

Riches, J., *Jesus and the Transformation of Judaism.* Darton, Longman & Todd, 1980.

Rist, J. M., *On the independence of Matthew and Mark.* Cambridge University, 1978

Rothfuchs, W., *Die Erfullungszitate des Matthäus-Evangeliums.* Stuttgart, Kohlhammer, 1969.

Rüger, H. P., "Mit welchem Mass ihr messt, wird euch gemessenwerden" (*Zeitschrift für die neutestamentliche Wissenschaft,* 1969).

Saldarini, A. J., "Johanan ben Zakkai's Escape from Jerusalem" (*Journal for the Study of Judaism,* 1975).

Sanders, E. P., *Paul and Palestinian Judaism.* SCM, 1977.

Schmid, J., *Das Evangelium nach Markus.* Regensburg, Pustet, 1954.

Smith, M., "A Comparison of Early Christian and Early Rabbinic Tradition" (*Journal of Biblical Literature,* 1963).

Stanton, G. N., "Bruce D. Chilton, *God in Strength*" (*Journal for the Study of the New Testament,* 1980).

——————, *Jesus of Nazareth in New Testament Preaching.* Cambridge University, 1974.

Steck, O. H., *Israel und das gewaltsame Geschick der Propheten.* Neukirchen, 1967.

Stein, R. H., "The 'Criteria' for Authenticity" in: France, R. T., and Wenham, D., eds., *Gospel Perspectives* I. JSOT, 1980.

Stendahl, K., *The School of St. Matthew.* Lund, Gleerup, 1954.

Stuhlmacher, P., *Historical Criticism and Theological Interpretation of Scripture.* SPCK, 1979.

Styler, G. M., "The Priority of Mark" in: Moule, C. F. D., *The Birth of the New Testament.* Black, 1981 (and previous editions).

Suhl, A., *Die Funktion der alttestamentlichen Zitate und Anspielungen im Markusevangelium.* Gütersloh, Mohn, 1965.

Tàrrech, A. P. "Lc 10:18: La visió de la Caiguda de Satanàs" (*Revista Catalana de Teologia*, 1978).

Trocmé, E., "Why Parables?" A Study of Mark IV" (*Bulletin of the John Rylands University Library of Manchester*, 1977).

Tuckett, C., "*God in Strength*" (*Scripture Bulletin*, 1980).

Turner, N., *A Grammar of New Testament Greek* IV. Clark, 1976.

Vermes, G., *Jesus the Jew.* Collins, 1973 (and reprints).

Walker, R., *Die Heilsgeschichte im ersten Evangelium.* Vandenhoeck & Ruprecht, 1967.

Weder, H., *Die Gleichnisse Jesu als Metaphern.* Vandenhoeck & Ruprecht, 1978.

Wieder, N., "The Habakkuk Scroll and the Targum" (*Journal of Jewish Studies*, 1953).

Wilcox, M., "The Promise of the 'Seed' in the New Testament and the Targumim" (*Journal for the Study of the New Testament*, 1979).

Wink, W., *John the Baptist in the Gospel Tradition*. Cambridge University, 1978.

York, A. D., "The Dating of the Targumic Literature" (*Journal for the Study of Judaism*, 1974).

Young, E. J., *The Book of Isaiah* II. Eerdmans, 1969.

Zimmermann, F., *The Aramaic Origin of the Four Gospels*. Ktav, 1979. (N.b., the author's name is misspelled on the cover and bibliography page; there are two "n's.")